FASHION

Fashion, an exploration of the murky waters o
RSC's The Other Place in April 1987. Thatche
Cash, self-made man and successful advertising
Tory Party account. To win it, he hires Stuart (
now fallen on hard times. Once the victim of Cl
controls his livelihood and, furthermore, is havir

'If, as someone in the play says, "advertising is the revenge of business upon culture" then this is also a revenge play.'

Paul Allen, *New Statesman*

'Lucie unnervingly depicts a complex, impenetrably manipulative world.'

Jim Hiley, *The Listener*

'Along the way there are deep thrusts into the heartlands of sexual politics. (Lucie is one of the few male playwrights to write fully-fledged, believable women's roles), a fascinating study of loneliness and some of the sharpest (and funniest) writing I've come across for a long time.'

Lyn Gardner, *City Limits*.

DOUG LUCIE was born in Chessington in 1953. He was Resident Playwright with the Oxford Playhouse Company from 1979-80 and worked as a Visiting Playwright to the University of Iowa, USA, in 1981. His plays include *John Clare's Mad Nuncle* (Edinburgh, 1975) *Rough Trade* (Oxford Playhouse, 1977), *We Love You* (Roundhouse, 1978), *Oh Well* (Oxford Playhouse, 1978), *The New Garbo* (Hull Truck and King's Head, London 1978), *Heroes* (Edinburgh and New End Theatre, London, 1979), *Fear of the Dark* (read by the RSC at the Royal Court Theatre Upstairs, 1980), *Poison* (Edinburgh Festival, 1980), *Strangers in the Night* (New End, 1981), *Hard Feelings* (Oxford Playhouse tour, 1982; Bush Theatre, London, 1983; BBC TV 1984), *Progress* (Bush, 1984), *Key to the World* (Paines Plough, Leicester Haymarket and Lyric Theatre Studio, Hammersmith, 1984) and *A Class of his Own* (BBC TV, 1984), *Force and Hypocrisy* (Young Vic Studio, 1986).

The photograph on the front cover shows Brian Cox as Paul Cash *in the Royal Shakespeare Company's production of* Fashion *at The Other Place (1987). It is reproduced by courtesy of Nobby Clark.*

in the same series

Karim Alrawi: A COLDER CLIMATE
Thomas Babe: BURIED INSIDE EXTRA
Aphra Behn: THE LUCKY CHANCE
Edward Bond: DEREK & CHORUSES FROM
   AFTER THE ASSASSINATIONS
   HUMAN CANNON
   THE WAR PLAYS: PARTS ONE & TWO
   THE WAR PLAYS: PART THREE
Howard Brenton: THE GENIUS
Howard Brenton (*A Short Sharp Shock!* written with
   Tony Howard): THIRTEENTH NIGHT & A
   SHORT SHARP SHOCK!
Howard Brenton and Tunde Ikoli: SLEEPING
   POLICEMEN
Mikhail Bulgakov (in a version by Dusty Hughes):
   MOLIÈRE
Edward Bulwer-Lytton: MONEY
Bob Carlton: RETURN TO THE FORBIDDEN
   PLANET
Jim Cartwright: ROAD
Anton Chekhov (in a version by Thomas Kilroy): THE
   SEAGULL
Caryl Churchill: SERIOUS MONEY
Caryl Churchill and David Lan: A MOUTHFUL OF
   BIRDS
Tony Craze, Ron Hart, Johnnie Quarrell: SHONA,
   LUNCH GIRLS, THE SHELTER
Sarah Daniels: BYRTHRITE
   NEAPTIDE
   RIPEN OUR DARKNESS & THE DEVIL'S
   GATEWAY
Nick Darke: THE BODY
   TING TANG MINE & OTHER PLAYS
David Edgar: WRECKERS
   ENTERTAINING STRANGERS
Harvey Fierstein: TORCH SONG TRILOGY
Peter Flannery: OUR FRIENDS IN THE NORTH
Peter Gibbs: RUMBLINGS
Nikolai Gogol (in a version by Adrian Mitchell): THE
   GOVERNMENT INSPECTOR
Robert Holman: MAKING NOISE QUIETLY
   OTHER WORLDS
   THE OVERGROWN PATH
   TODAY
Debbie Horsfield: THE RED DEVILS TRILOGY
Ron Hutchinson: RAT IN THE SKULL
Henrik Ibsen (translated by David Rudkin): PEER
   GYNT
Terry Johnson: CRIES FROM THE MAMMAL
   HOUSE
   INSIGNIFICANCE
Terry Johnson and Kate Lock: TUESDAY'S CHILD
   & TIME TROUBLE
Charlotte Keatley: MY MOTHER SAID I NEVER
   SHOULD
Barrie Keeffe: BASTARD ANGEL
   BETTER TIMES
   SUS
Paul Kember: NOT QUITE JERUSALEM
Hanif Kureishi: BORDERLINE
David Lan: FLIGHT
Deborah Levy: HERESIES

Stephen Lowe: TOUCHED
   TIBETAN INROADS
   MOVING PICTURES
   (*Moving Pictures, Seeing Stars, Strive*)
Doug Lucie: PROGRESS & HARD FEELINGS
John Mackendrick: LAVENDER BLUE & NOLI
   ME TANGERE
David Mamet: EDMOND
Tony Marchant: THICK AS THIEVES
   WELCOME HOME, RASPBERRY, THE LUCKY
   ONES
Philip Massinger: A NEW WAY TO PAY OLD
   DEBTS
Mustapha Matura: PLAY MAS, INDEPENDENCE
   & MEETINGS
Michael Meyer: LUNATIC AND LOVER
Anthony Minghella: MADE IN BANGKOK
   WHALE MUSIC & OTHER PLAYS
G.F. Newman: OPERATION BAD APPLE
   AN HONOURABLE TRADE
Louise Page: BEAUTY AND THE BEAST
   REAL ESTATE
   SALONIKA
Harold Pinter: ONE FOR THE ROAD
Stephen Poliakoff: STRAWBERRY FIELDS
   SHOUT ACROSS THE RIVER
   AMERICAN DAYS
   THE SUMMER PARTY
   FAVOURITE NIGHTS & CAUGHT ON A
   TRAIN
   RUNNERS & SOFT TARGETS
Christina Reid: JOYRIDERS & TEA IN A
   CHINA CUP
William Saroyan: THE TIME OF YOUR LIFE
Ntozake Shange: SPELL NUMBER SEVEN
Wallace Shawn (*My Dinner with Andre* written with
   Andre Gregory): AUNT DAN AND LEMON
   MY DINNER WITH ANDRE & MARIE AND
   BRUCE
C.P. Taylor: LIVE THEATRE. Four Plays for Young
   People
Sue Townsend: BAZAAR AND RUMMAGE,
   GROPING FOR WORDS & WOMBERANG
   THE GREAT CELESTIAL COW
Michelene Wandor and Mike Alfreds:
   THE WANDERING JEW
Peter Whelan: CLAY
Edgar White: THE NINE NIGHT & RITUAL BY
   WATER
Michael Wilcox: RENTS
   LENT
   MASSAGE & OTHER PLAYS
Nigel Williams: SUGAR AND SPICE & TRIAL
   RUN
   W.C.P.C.
Snoo Wilson: THE GRASS WIDOW
Charles Wood: HAS 'WASHINGTON' LEGS? &
   DINGO
Nicholas Wright: THE DESERT AIR
   CUSTOM OF THE COUNTRY

FASHION

DOUG LUCIE

A METHUEN PAPERBACK

A METHUEN NEW THEATRESCRIPT

First published in Great Britain as a paperback original in the
Methuen New Theatrescript series in 1987 by
Methuen London Ltd., 11 New Fetter Lane, London EC4P 4EE
and in the United States of America by
Methuen Inc., 29 West 35th Street, New York NY 10001

Photoset in 9pt Times by 𝙵\Tek Art Ltd, Croydon, Surrey
Printed in Great Britain by Richard Clay Ltd, Bungay, Suffolk

British Library Cataloguing in Publication Data

Lucie, Doug
    Fashion. — (A Methuen new theatrescript).
    I. Title
    822'.914   PR6062.U1/

    ISBN 0-413-17200-7

CAUTION

For Cathy and Linda

Fashion was first presented by the Royal Shakespeare Company at The Other Place, Stratford-upon-Avon, on 7 April 1987, with the following cast:

PAUL CASH — Brian Cox
LIZ SCOULER — Stella Gonet
ROBIN GINGHAM — Akim Mokaji
STUART CLARKE — Alun Armstrong
ERIC BRIGHT — Clive Russell
HOWARD LAMPETER — David Honey
AMANDA CLARKE — Estelle Kohler
DOOLEY — David O'Hara
GILLIAN HUNTLEY — Linda Spurrier

Directed by Nick Hamm
Set design by Fotini Dimou
Lighting by Ian Loffhagen
Sound by Mo Weinstock
Fights by Malcolm Ransom

ACT ONE

Scene One

6.40 a.m. A plush office on the top floor of a building in a quiet back street in central London. The set is split level. The lower, office level is hi-tech: desk, sofa, chairs, hi-fi, large video screen. The upper level is a modern kitchen and dining area, with a pine table and chairs. To one side of the set is a glass door leading to the lobby where the reception desk is.

On the sofa, we can just make out a blurred shape. It is PAUL CASH asleep in a sleeping bag.

A telephone rings once and the answering machine clicks on. All phone calls are amplified round the office on a speaker. When CASH uses the phone, he has one he can use without needing to use the receiver, so he can hold a conversation almost anywhere in the room.

The voice on the answering machine tape is that of LIZ SCOULER, CASH's secretary.

LIZ: Hello, Cash Creative Consultancy. There's nobody in the office at the moment, but if you'd like to leave your name and number, we'll get back to you as soon as possible. Thank you for calling. (*The tone sounds.*)

BERKOWITZ: Hi, Cash. Berkowitz, New York. Listen, I just finished with McLeish and Harper, and thank God, the landscape's starting to flatten out at last. They bit on Windfall and the TCC promo, but I have to tell you, Gingham's five-part went down like cold cockroach chilli. You see who we're getting in the sack with here. The Guggenheim Foundation it ain't. Anyhow, two for three's an OK strike rate. And hey, listen, Buckley's still chewing me out over the visit. See what you can do, huh? Dinner at Downing Street is top option, but I know how these things are. It'd sure grease the wheels, anyhow. Oh, yeah, you can reach me at the Boston office after tomorrow a.m. OK? Ciao.

The phone line goes off. CASH slowly gets out of the sleeping bag, naked. He sits for a moment, scratching, stretches, stands up and walks across to the answering machine and presses the button to rewind the tape. On the desk are last night's Chinese takeaway containers. He picks up a spoon and eats some cold Chinese food, then goes to the drinks cabinet and pours a mineral water. The tape has rewound. He switches it on. As it plays, he takes two hand weights from under the sofa and does lifting exercises and t'ai chi style movement and breathing. The first call is from HOWARD.

HOWARD: Hello, Paul. Howard. Ten-thirty p.m. Tuesday. Sorry not to get back to you earlier. Got stuck in a bloody briefing at Number Ten. Twerp from the *New Statesman*'s got hold of some defence leak. End of civilisation as we etcetera. Honestly, what a bunch of tossers. Of course they'll all be rounded up if there's a nuclear alert, what on earth do they bloody well expect? Still, page and a half in the *New Statesman*, thirty seconds on Channel Four News, total audience figures: two lesbians, a dog and Tony Benn. Anyway, the matter in hand. I have a cautious green light. So see what you and our dusky chum can magic up for me. OK? And listen, it's not entirely a matter of public record just yet, so complete discretion would be appreciated. Right. Talk, or lunch or something. Better still, I'll pop in. I'm on grooming duty with one of our new candidates, so you should meet her before we do the presentation chat. All right? Over and out.

The tape beeps and goes on to the next call which is from ERIC BRIGHT.

ERIC: Paul, it's Eric Bright, returning your call returning my call. Yes, Wednesday, ten-thirty would be fine. Bye.

The tape beeps and goes on to the next call, which is from STUART CLARKE. He is drunk.

STUART: Cash, you bastard? It's Stuart. Old Clarkie. Listen, you creep, why can't you return my calls? Eh? I've left you three bloody messages in a week. So come on. You know I'm the best director you're going to get. Give me a job. Any job. I'm not proud. Hovis, Andrex, the wonder of sodding

Woolworths, I don't care. Just employ me, right? We go back a long way, Cash, so shuffle some of that green folding stuff my way, or I'll come round there and break your teeth. (*Beat. He belches.*) Oh, and Amanda sends her love.

The tape beeps and goes on to the next call, which is from a young Scottish man.

MAN: I know you. (CASH *stiffens slightly.*) Yeah. I know you all right. Nancy boy. Nonce. (*Beat.*) Thought it was a secret, didn't you? Well, it's not. 'Cos I know. (*Beat.*) I'll bet you're trying to put a face to my voice now, aren't you? A *pretty* wee face. (*Beat.*) Well, fret not. You'll get your chance. In the flesh. (*Beat.*) Is it nice up there in your castle? Eh? Thick carpets? Leather chairs? Money pasted all over the walls? The smell of lovely money? (*Beat.*) I'm coming. I'm going to invade your space. Soon. Bye bye. Darling.

He blows a kiss and puts the phone down. This is the last call. The tape runs on silently. CASH puts the weights away. He saunters over and switches off the answering machine, opens a desk diary, finds a phone number and dials. It rings for a long time. Finally it's answered. It is AMANDA CLARKE.

AMANDA (*half-asleep*): Hello?

CASH: Amanda, hello, darling.

AMANDA: What? Paul, is that you?

CASH: Yes. (*Beat.*)

AMANDA: Are you all right?

CASH: Fine. (*Beat.*)

AMANDA: What time is it?

CASH: Six-forty.

AMANDA: Uh huh. (*Beat.*) Well?

CASH: Oh, what are you doing for dinner tonight?

AMANDA: Are you kidding?

CASH: No.

AMANDA: Actually, I'm busy. Maxwell's in town, so my arse has to be well in gear.

CASH: Never mind. Let me talk to your husband, will you?

AMANDA: Stuart?

CASH: That's the one. Unless there's something you haven't told me.

AMANDA: I don't know where he is. Last time I saw him, he was popping out for a drink. Three days ago . . . oh, hang on, his coat's here. I'll see if I can find him.

Pause, during which CASH takes out an electric razor and starts to shave. AMANDA comes back.

Hello, Paul?

He switches off the razor.

He's on the sofa with a bottle of Jack Daniels. I've woken him up. What d'you want him for?

CASH: I'm just returning his call.

AMANDA: You bastard. (*Beat.*) I'm going to take a shower, now I'm awake.

CASH: Wish I could be there.

AMANDA: Yeah. (*Beat.*) Look, I may give you a ring at lunch, OK?

CASH: OK.

Pause, during which CASH starts shaving again. STUART comes to the phone.

STUART: Cash? (CASH *stops shaving.*)

CASH: Hang on a minute, will you, Stuart? (*He finishes shaving.*) Right.(*Beat.*) How are you?

STUART: For fuck's sake, man, you don't ring me at this time of day to ask how I am.

CASH: Never did have much time for the formal niceties, did you?

STUART: Bollocks.

CASH: Still the angry young man.

STUART: No, I've matured. I'm now a slightly peeved young middle-aged man. With a terrible fucking hangover. So what is it?

CASH: *You've* been ringing *me*, Clarke. I don't need this. (*He hangs up, goes over to the sleeping bag and folds it up. The phone rings. He flips the switch on the desk.*) Cash.

AMANDA: Paul, what are you playing at? You ring at the crack of dawn and hang up . . .

CASH: Listen, darling, some of us get up early. That's why some of us are very successful. On the other hand, some of us spend our lives in an alcoholic stupor. Which is why some of us are no-hope ex-movie directors.

AMANDA: Paul . . .

CASH: But, seeing as Stuart's an old friend, and seeing as he's been leaving begging messages on my answering machine, and seeing as I'm screwing his wife behind his back, I thought I might help him out. Put a bit of work his way. Just like you wanted. Remember? (*Beat.*) However, when I call him to tell him the good news about his career prospects, all I get is the usual fucking mouthful. And so I hang up. (*Beat.*) And I can smell his breath from here. I thought you said he'd got it under control.

AMANDA: He had when I last looked.

CASH: When was that?

AMANDA: I don't remember.

CASH: Well, you should look more often.

AMANDA: What? No fear. (*Beat.*) Actually, he had a little bit of money through, so he went on a bender. (*Beat.*)

CASH. Just put him back on, will you?

AMANDA: OK.

She goes away from the phone and we hear her call 'Stuart' etc. Suddenly the lights in the office come on. CASH doesn't react. We see LIZ SCOULER going into the lobby towards the reception desk in her coat. She disappears. She comes back across by the door, coat in hand, to hang it up. CASH drops the food containers in the waste bin. STUART comes to the phone.

STUART. Hello.

CASH. Let's start again, shall we?

STUART: Yeah. (*Beat.*)

CASH: Tell me, Stuart, do you still subjugate your art to your politics?

STUART: Christ's sake, Cash . . .

CASH: What I mean is, do you still refuse to produce work which you consider to be detrimental to the interests of the proletariat?

STUART: I don't get the chance. I don't produce. Remember?

CASH: Well really, Clarkie, a film with an Arab hero is a touch near the knuckle. A Palestinian Arab hero . . . that's a fucking suicide note. (*Beat.*) Anyway, I need to know whether you're politically a little bit more flexible these days.

STUART: Isn't everybody? (*Beat.*) Try me.

LIZ enters with a small bowl, flannel and towel. She puts it on the desk by CASH. They don't acknowledge each other. LIZ goes. CASH washes and dries his face through the following conversation.

CASH: What I want to know, Stuart, is if I employ you on a specific campaign, would you allow your personal – sorry, ideological – feelings to interfere with your work?

STUART: Depends.

CASH: No. Let's have no grey areas. I want it cut and dried, black and white. Are you a professional director, or a professional liberal?

STUART: I've never been a liberal. You know that.

CASH: How very true.

LIZ comes back in with CASH's clothes for the day. Suit, shirt, tie, socks, underwear. She lays them out on the sofa and goes, taking the sleeping bag.

STUART: One thing I do know. You've got to be a realist to survive. So, if you want it straight, yeah, I'll do the work, whatever.

CASH: Glad to see you've adjusted to the spirit of the time.

STUART: No one said it's going to last for ever. It's not as if we're talking about the thousand-year Reich. I hope.

LIZ comes in and goes up to the kitchen and prepares coffee and orange juice. CASH *opens his desk diary.*

CASH: OK, I want you here this morning. Say ten.

STUART: Oh God . . .

CASH: Realism, Stuart . . .

STUART. Yeah. I'll be there. Listen, I think Amanda wants to speak to you. Dinner invite or something.

CASH: OK. See you at ten.

STUART: Yeah. (*Pause while* AMANDA *comes to the phone.*)

AMANDA: Paul?

CASH: Hi.

AMANDA: Look, I thought, seeing as you'd called, we could arrange . . . (*Beat.*) It's OK, he's gone. (LIZ *looks round.* AMANDA *speaks softly.*) So?

CASH: He's coming in.

AMANDA: Thanks. (*Beat.*) I'm sure you can use him. We both know how good he is.

CASH: Was, darling.

AMANDA: You don't lose something that special. (*Beat.*) If you want to meet up tonight, we could always go for a nightcap at the Bluebird.

CASH: Sounds good.

AMANDA: Maybe you deserve a treat. (*Beat.*) Speak to you later.

CASH: Bye.

AMANDA: Bye.

He flips the switch and goes over to his clothes and starts to dress.

LIZ: Good morning, Mr Cash.

CASH: Good morning, Liz.

LIZ: D'you want toast?

CASH: No thanks.

LIZ: Cereal?

CASH: No.

LIZ: You'll get an ulcer. Or worse. Bowel cancer. That's terrible. And it's real common.

CASH: So I hear.

LIZ: I'll just do you a small bowl then, shall I?

CASH: Why not?

LIZ (*doing the cereal*): Don't want you wasting away, do we?

CASH: Not much chance of that.

LIZ: It happens really quickly. Like my dad. he got so skinny you could see the bones. Like one of them concentration camp people. (*She puts the cereal on the desk.*) There. And eat it all up.

CASH: Keep me clear till lunch, Liz. Eric Bright should be in mid-morning, and I've got someone coming in at ten.

LIZ: Right.

CASH: And have Robin clear his desk for the day. I'm going to need him.

LIZ: What about calls?

CASH: No domestic. Only US and SA. Message if you can. And if Amanda calls this morning while there's anybody with me, definitely take a message.

LIZ: Uh huh. (*She opens the window blinds. Light floods in.*) It's a beautiful day. (CASH *is dressed. He buttons his jacket and sits at his desk.*)

CASH: What?

LIZ: It's a beautiful day. (*Beat.*)

CASH: Every day's a beautiful day, Liz. Every day. (*She turns and half smiles.*)

Blackout.

Scene Two

The office, about 9.45 the same morning. It is deserted. Pause. ROBIN GINGHAM *enters, just arrived for work. He's eating an apple. He goes to the kitchen area and pours a coffee, then comes down to* CASH's *desk and browses through some papers on it.* LIZ *enters.*

LIZ: Good morning, Mr Gingham. (*He starts slightly.*)

ROBIN: Oh, hi Liz. (*She tidies the papers up.*) State secrets? (*She smiles professionally.*) Where's sir?

LIZ: Popped out.

ROBIN: What? Out of his office? Out of . . . the building? Christ. Have we had the four-minute warning, or is his bank on fire?

LIZ: He's gone to buy a shirt.

ROBIN: The plot thickens.

LIZ: He spilled coffee down the one he had on.

ROBIN: Ah. (*Beat.*) Liz, do you ever have, like, really silly thoughts?

LIZ: No.

ROBIN: I thought not.

LIZ: I'm a secretary.

Beat while he ponders this for a moment. She starts to go. He calls her back.

ROBIN: Liz.

LIZ: Yes?

ROBIN: Cardinal Richelieu died in 1642. (*Beat.*) Thought you might like to know.

LIZ: Thank you. Mr Cash wants you to keep yourself free today.

ROBIN: For what?

LIZ: Work?

ROBIN: Hey, careful, I had a heavy night.

LIZ: There are people coming in this morning. The Smith Square account, I think.

ROBIN: Ah. Indeed. Work.(*Beat.*) Have we got the account then?

LIZ: I don't know.

ROBIN: So who's coming in?

LIZ: I don't know.

ROBIN: What's the only mammal that can't jump? (*Beat.*)

LIZ: The elephant. (*She turns and goes as* CASH *comes in with his new shirt.*)

CASH: Rob.

ROBIN: Hi.

CASH (*changing his shirt*): Stan Berkowitz called.

ROBIN: The Beast of the Bronx. What'd he have to say?

CASH: They loved Windfall and TCC.

ROBIN: Hacks.

CASH: And they found your grand opus . . .

ROBIN: Yuh?

CASH: A crock of shit, darling. (*Beat.*) No reason as yet. (*Beat.*) *I* liked it.

ROBIN: Paul, why do we work for these jerks? I mean, that's the third biggie they've nixed.

CASH: We'll get there.

ROBIN: Christ, I spent nearly two weeks getting that bastard looking right. And it looks bloody perfect. That promotion's a work of art, for Christ's sake. (*Beat.*)

CASH: Rob, I've told you: advertising is the revenge of business on culture. We inform, we entertain, but most of all, we oil the wheels of commerce.

ROBIN. Paul, people are image-sophisticated. They read the messages loud and clear. The most snotty-nosed tower block kid can recognise Russia in a Levi's ad. References stretching back through Le Carré, *Ipcress*, Tarkovsky, *The Twilight Zone*, Dostoevsky, James Dean. Every advert thirty seconds of cinematic purity. Claude Chabrol with Persil in the starring role. People *know*. They're sussed, Paul.

CASH: Not so McLeish and Harper. (*Quickly, he doesn't want to have this conversation.*) Look, we've market tested, we've random sampled, we've pinpointed our target group. Now all we have to do is convince the Yanks we can come up with the package to sell to that group. Easy, really. So fuck art. Let's make money. (*Beat.* ROBIN *smiles.*)

ROBIN: Whatever you say.

CASH: I'd never have put your idea in if I hadn't believed in it. Honestly.

ROBIN: Yeah. (*Beat.*) I have this fantasy, right? We're filming for a new shampoo, and on the studio floor we've got . . . I dunno . . . Redgrave and Irons, with Menges and Joffe behind the camera, and in the corner, doing a rewrite, there's Stoppard and Shaffer. Don't tell me that wouldn't make money.

CASH: Did the British film industry?

(*Beat.*) How's the script coming on, by the way? (ROBIN *is evasive.*)

ROBIN: How did yours come on?

CASH: Got as far as the title page.

ROBIN: I haven't even got that far.

CASH: It'll come.

ROBIN: Yours didn't.

CASH: I got sidetracked.

ROBIN: Me too. D'you know what I mean? I go back to that nice piece of real estate I call home, and I sit there and I think, right, Robin old son, let's make like Hollywood. Let's do the Putnam shuffle. And I come up with three brilliant ideas, and I pour a nice long writer's drink and I visualise these great movies. They are so good. So I decide I have to tell somebody, go out, get absolutely plastered and end up playing Trivial Pursuit till the sun comes up. I've got visualisation and I've got realisation. It's just the intervening period of creation that's absent.

CASH: And I thought you took your *work* home with you.

ROBIN: Bollocks, boss. Ahem, talking of which, what's this Liz tells me about Smith Square?

CASH: I'm not absolutely sure yet. I'm just putting some people together, see what happens, see if we can't get a little piece of the action.

ROBIN: I thought it was all sewn up.

CASH: Not entirely. Mind you, how could they resist? We have genius on our side.

ROBIN: Why, thank you.

CASH: I meant me. (*They exchange a smile.*) Anyway, Eric's coming in later. (*He looks at his watch.*) And I've got a director coming in any minute.

ROBIN: Anybody I know?

CASH: Could be. So . . . thinking cap time. I want to see you sparkle.

ROBIN: OK. I'll just make a couple of calls.

CASH: Fine. (ROBIN *goes as* LIZ *comes in with some letters to be signed.*) Coffee, Liz. (*She goes to the kitchen.*)

Strong. And can you get on to Rodney, tell him that if Benson keeps stalling we'll have to take him to court.

As he speaks, STUART CLARKE *comes into reception. He stands a moment and looks around.*

And send him a copy of the figures. Just in case the last lot got lost in the post.

LIZ: I understand Mr Benson has cash flow problems.

STUART *is thinking about coming into the office.*

CASH: This is not an episode of *Minder*, Liz. Mr Benson's chirpy cockney patois will not excuse the fact that he owes me seventeen grand.

STUART *stands gingerly in the doorway. He takes a deep breath, knocks on the door and strides in very purposefully.*

STUART. Cash, you old bastard.

CASH: Stuart. (*They greet each other with a warm but tentative hand shake.*) Long time, long time. (*Then* STUART *holds out his arms and they embrace, still tentative.*) How are you?

STUART: Great, y'know . . .

CASH: Yeah, you've put on weight.

STUART: Idle living.

CASH: Couple of games of squash, I'll soon sort you out.

STUART: Make that five card draw and you're on.

CASH: Times *have* changed.

STUART: Yeah. They have. (*Beat.*)

CASH: Uh, that's Liz. My secretary and saviour.

STUART: Hello, Liz.

LIZ: Hello.

CASH: Is that coffee ready?

LIZ: Nearly.

CASH (*going to the kitchen*): Strong, black. I'm guessing here . . .

STUART: Spot on.

CASH: How's Amanda? (LIZ *looks at him.*)

STUART: You tell me. (CASH *stiffens*.) I've hardly spoken to her for a month.

CASH: Diverging lifestyles . . .

STUART: No, she hates my guts. (*Beat.*) Hey, I have to thank you.

CASH: For what?

STUART: For opening my eyes to a new cultural experience.

LIZ *has poured the coffee, which* CASH *brings down to* STUART. LIZ *goes.*

CASH: I have?

STUART: Yeah. Y'know, before this morning, when you summoned me here for this dawn rendezvous, I had never seen, that is to say, I had gone out of my way to avoid seeing, breakfast television. And now . . . well, what can I say? Except: mine eyes have seen the Glory of the Cardie of Frank Bough. I have a deep-seated and probably totally irrational dislike of the man. The Torquemada of the telly, Little England's revenge.

CASH: Actually, he's terribly chummy. (*Beat.*) I've been on.

STUART: What, on breakfast TV?

CASH: Yes.

STUART: Fuck me. (*Beat.*) Odd really; we inherit these poxy Yank broadcasting traditions, the chat show, the game show breakfast TV and we render them totally and predictably English. Watching TV these days is like flicking through those magazines you get in the waiting room at the clap clinic. A boring diversion whilst awaiting the dreadful news. Which never comes. (*Beat.*) I ask you, who in their right mind wants to watch that first thing in the morning? Who in their right mind even wants to be up at that time of the day?

CASH: The masses?

STUART: Oh, them. (*Beat.*)

CASH: Here, sit down. (*They sit.*) Got a lot to catch up on.

STUART: Yeah. (*Beat.*) Sorry about the phone calls.

CASH: Not at all. Breath of fresh air.

STUART: No, I was soused.

CASH: The way I remember it, you always were.

STUART: No. That was energy. But . . . you get older, the energy flags, the drink talks. (*Beat.*) Cash, I'm up for it. I need to work.

CASH: Money problems?

STUART (*lying*): Not really. I still get a few bob from the old stuff. And Amanda's very good, y'know . . .

CASH: Done any work?

STUART (*laughs*): Home video.

CASH: Ah. Let's not talk about that, then.

STUART: Not the hard stuff. Just . . . I dunno, women with no clothes on. Cadbury's Flake without the Flake, if you know what I mean.

CASH: Yeah. (*Beat.*) Look, I can't promise on this particular project, it's all up in the air at the moment, but if it doesn't work out, there's other stuff I could consider you for.

STUART: Thanks.

CASH: And if it does work out, I'm doing myself a favour. You've been out in the cold for too long now.

STUART: I'm not into a comeback. I just want to work.

CASH: I know. (*Beat.*) God, this is funny isn't it? Fifteen, twenty years ago, you were up there. You commanded the heights. People like me . . . well . . .

STUART: You were into money.

CASH: I know. The lowest of the low. Completely ruined my sex life. Politics and art were sexy. Money and work were a cold shower. While you were making those movies . . . great movies, I might say . . . and enjoying the fruits thereof, I was on my own, tossing off and dreaming of this.

STUART: And tell me, Mr Cash, when did you *stop* beating your meat? (*Beat.*) Sorry. I'm here for a job. I better shut up.

CASH: No. What I mean is . . . things are very different now. *This* is sexy.

STUART: You're making me feel old.

CASH: No, not old. Old-fashioned.

STUART: Fashions change. Today the miniskirt, tomorrow trouser suits.

CASH: Don't underestimate it. The one constant is that it's always there. You were fashionable once. Be grateful. (*Beat.*) Lecture over.

STUART: No, feel free. I seem to remember haranguing you at every available opportunity in the old days.

CASH: That's true. You threw me out of the house once.

STUART: God, did I?

CASH: Uh huh. Called me a despicable Tory anarchist and shoved me down the steps.

STUART: I remember.

CASH: And I shouted: hey, less of the anarchist if you don't mind.

STUART: I don't remember that.

CASH (*icy*): No. You'd slammed the door by that time. (*Beat.*) I could hear you all laughing inside. Amanda, Maggie, John, Freddy, I think was there . . .

STUART: The three-day week. It was then.

CASH: Yeah. Candles.

STUART: One thing about Ted Heath: he knew how to lend atmosphere to a dinner party.

CASH: It's more than I did.

STUART: Not true. You provided us with some very entertaining moments.

CASH: I *am* glad. (*Beat.*) Anyway, that's all in the past.

STUART: So what's in the present?

CASH: Right. I've got a very specific proposition to put to you. It's not definite yet, but if we get it, it's big. If we don't get it, you'll still receive a development fee. Sound OK?

STUART: Why me?

CASH: I went down the BFI last week. Had a look at some of your old stuff. Some of that work is incredible. Just the camera work. Brilliant. Incredibly powerful.

STUART: Thank you.

CASH: It's true. (*Beat.*) And that's what I need. Something unashamedly manipulative. Emotive.

STUART: In what sort of area? (*Beat.*)

CASH: Propaganda. Stuart, I want to make the sort of film that, were he alive today, Goebbels would be making. (*Beat.*)

STUART: I see. And who exactly would be exploiting my talents for this little trip down memory lane? (*Beat.*)

CASH: The Conservative Party.

STUART: What?

CASH: We're looking at the chance to produce the next four Tory party political broadcasts. (*Beat.* ROBIN *comes in.*) Ah, Robin, great. Robin, this is Stuart Clarke. Robin's my chief partner in crime. Stuart. Well, not quite partner yet. (ROBIN *holds his hand out.* STUART *has stood up. He stares at* CASH.)

STUART: You absolute fucking toerag. (*Beat.*) You arsehole. (ROBIN *has withdrawn his hand.*) Yeah. Good, game, Cash. I'll be seeing you.

CASH: Stuart . . .

STUART *turns round.*

STUART: Don't mate. Let me go, then you can have your little laugh.

CASH: I won't be laughing if you go.

STUART: No?

CASH: No. If I wanted to humiliate you, I could do it in a million ways. Sorry, but it's true. I never joke about work. (STUART *considers his next move.*) Have another coffee.

CASH *nods at* ROBIN, *who takes* STUART's *cup to the kitchen and fills it.*

Black.

ROBIN: Hmmm?

CASH: The coffee.

ROBIN *brings* STUART *his coffee.* STUART *takes out a quarter bottle of*

Scotch and pours some into his cup. He drinks, daring CASH *to say something. He sits again.*

STUART: Right. So what makes you think a socialist director who hasn't made a film in six years is the right person to produce films for the Tory Party?

CASH: Simple. I want the best.

STUART: How the fuck d'you expect me to work for the people my whole professional life's been spent trying to expose?

CASH: This is work. Not art. Skill. Not passion. (*Beat.*) Look, Stuart, I have a reputation for making things happen. Things people thought were impossible. Come on. Let's do the impossible. (*Beat.*) I happen to think that the idea of you making Tory broadcasts is mind-bogglingly brilliant. (*Beat.*)

STUART: I suppose if I turn this down, I don't get another chance.

CASH: That's right, yes. (*Beat.*) It's an interesting team. You won't be the only renegade socialist.

STUART: Oh? Dug up Ramsay MacDonald, have you?

CASH: Close.

STUART: Who?

CASH: Ex-Labour MP. Now a TV pundit and newspaper columnist . . . (*Beat.*)

STUART: Eric Bright.

CASH: On the button.

STUART: Eric sodding Bright. I can't work with that schmuck.

CASH: Why not?

STUART: Christ, if we all moved to the right as fast as he did, we'd knock the earth off its axis. (ROBIN *sighs heavily.*) Sorry?

ROBIN: Politics are boring.

STUART: Oh, it talks then.

CASH: Rather well.

STUART: Does it ever think? Or is *that* too boring?

ROBIN: I don't know what it is, but whenever I encounter a sixties has-been flaunting his political soul, I come over all lethargic.

STUART: This boy of yours any good?

CASH: Very.

STUART: He'll have to be if he wants to get away with talking to me like that. (ROBIN *smirks.* STUART *turns to* CASH.) D'you remember that time . . . God, where was it . . . the Chinese place. That Tory prat. Remember?

CASH: Yeah.

STUART: Gave us a lecture on the evils of socialism. Said I should be shot. (*He smiles.*) Looked a bit funny, didn't he, when I broke his nose. (*Beat.*)

ROBIN: Wow. Right on. You break a guy's nose because he has different politics to you. Highly egalitarian.

STUART: No, I broke his nose because he knocked my drink over and refused to buy me another one. See, there's only one thing I hate more than a Tory, and that's a graceless Tory. (*Beat.*)

CASH: I want you in on this one Stuart. And I have to tell you, it feels good. (*Beat.*) D'you want a bit of time? Think it over?

STUART *looks at him glumly and shakes his head.*

STUART: No. No thanks.

Beat. Then he holds out his hand to ROBIN, *smiling.*

Hello, Robin. I understand we're going to be working together.

They shake.

Blackout.

Scene Three

Lunchtime the same day. STUART *is sitting on the sofa, a near-empty bottle of wine on the table, and a half-eaten salad on his lap.* LIZ *is washing up in the kitchen. She seems half-nervous and half-pitying of him.*

LIZ: Is there anything I can get for you, Mr Clarke?

He drains his glass.

STUART: Some more of this stuff, if you've got it. (*She goes to the fridge and gets another bottle and starts to uncork it.*) I hope it's bloody expensive.

LIZ: D'you like it?

STUART: Only if it costs. That's the point, isn't it?

LIZ: Is it?

STUART: That's what I thought. (*Beat.*) Unless I'm out of touch. (*She brings the bottle down to him.*)

LIZ: Actually, it's £1.99 a bottle. Mr Cash gets a discount.

STUART: I'll bet he does. Tell you what, I'll have a brandy.

LIZ: Och . . .

STUART: A large one. (*Beat, she seems to want to say something.*) I've heard it all before, Liz, so don't waste your breath.

LIZ: I wouldn't bother. I've *seen* it all before. (*She goes back to the kitchen and pours a brandy.*)

STUART: Thanks for the lunch, anyway.

LIZ: 'S OK.

STUART: It was very healthy. (*She brings the brandy.*)

LIZ: Who is it you're punishing?

STUART: Oh no, please . . .

LIZ: It's somebody. I know in the long run it's you, but that's not where it started, is it?

STUART: Look, I'll only say this once. Mind your own fucking business.

LIZ: Then get your own fucking brandy. (*She takes it back.*)

STUART (*laughing, trying to shrug it off*): OK, I'm sorry. Peace? (*She puts the glass down in the kitchen and stands defiant.*) It's not somebody. It's *some*thing. (*He goes and gets the glass.*)

LIZ: Aye. That's what they always say. (*Beat.*) Why are drunks so predictable? Eh? I mean, you can take a hundred people, all completely different, and then you get them drunk, and they all turn into the same person. (*Beat.*)

There was a documentary on the other night. Australian aborigines. They looked incredible, y'know? But they've given them drink, and Coca-Cola T-shirts and cut-off jeans, and now they look like every wino you ever saw in your life before. It was heartbreaking. (*Beat.*)

STUART: Isn't Cash responsible for some lager accounts?

LIZ: Aye. And vodka, and French liquers. (*Beat.*) But Mr Cash only drinks mineral water.

STUART: Mais naturellement. (*He smiles.*)

LIZ: You know what happens to alcoholic men? Their breasts swell and their testicles shrink. (*Beat.*)

STUART: What about women?

LIZ: They've already had the experience. (*He pours another drink.*)

STUART: Don't you have any vices then, Liz?

LIZ: Oh aye. Men.

STUART: Sorry, can't help you there. I'm a one-woman man. (*She gives him a sorry look.*)

LIZ: I like Arab men, anyway.

STUART: Ah.

LIZ: My weakness. (*Beat.*)

STUART: You and . . . what's his name . . .?

LIZ: Who? Robin? No way. He's more English than strawberries at Wimbledon. He's just a boy, in any case. I value finesse. (*He raises his glass.*)

STUART: To quality.

ERIC BRIGHT *suddenly comes in, cheerful and lively.*

ERIC: Hullo, Liz. Little bit on the late side, I'm afraid. Couldn't be helped.

LIZ: Mr Cash is in Mr Gingham's office looking at some artwork. He won't be long.

ERIC: Smashing.

LIZ: I'll tell him you're here.

ERIC: That's smashing.

She goes out. STUART *studies the label on the brandy bottle as* ERIC *goes to the kitchen and opens the fridge. He opens a bottle of Guinness and pours, lovingly.*

Nectar of the gods. Dublin-brewed. Nothing like it. A glassful of history. Cheerio.

He drinks and smacks his lips. STUART *studies his glass.*

STUART: French. Overpriced. Somebody else's. A goblet of bile. (*He knocks it back.*)

ERIC (*busying himself with his case*): Waiting for Paul, are you?

STUART: Liz does the waiting. I'm a guest. (*Beat.* ERIC *smiles.*)

ERIC: Yes. But seriously.

STUART: Hmmm?

ERIC: Are we part of the same affair?

STUART: I sincerely hope not. We haven't been properly introduced.

ERIC: I sort of assumed you'd know who I was.

STUART: Yes, but I'm a stickler for protocol. (*Beat.*)

ERIC: Eric Bright.

STUART: We've met.

ERIC: Really? When?

STUART: Nineteen seventy . . . six. The terrace at the House of Commons. Photocall.

ERIC: Ah. Photographer, are you?

STUART: No. (*Beat.*) Arts for Labour. I was an artist. For Labour. You were an MP. For Labour.

ERIC: Don't remind me. (*Beat.*) I'm sorry . . . you're . . .?

STUART: Stuart Clarke. (*Beat.*) Films. *Red Sky over Clydeside? The Poacher*?

ERIC: Of course, yes. I remember. Haven't done a lot this, er, decade, have you?

STUART: I was before my time. Tragic.

ERIC: Yes, yes   Arts for Labour. I was there, was I?

STUART: In body, at least.

ERIC: That's right. One of the problems with Labour, isn't it? We could always get Arts for the Party. Demonstrators for the Party, pop groups for the Party. It was *votes* for the Party where we came unstuck. (*Beat.*) Yes, I remember it now. Jim Callaghan was petrified somebody was going to smoke pot like the Beatles at Buck House. In fact, they were a very . . . respectable lot. Crusty even. Yourself excepted, of course. The electorate must have thought they were being asked to return the cast of *Coronation Street* to Number Ten.

STUART: Instead, they opted for *Miami Vice*.

ERIC: And who's to say they were wrong?

STUART: Not you, I'll bet.

ERIC: This is a democracy. The people made their choice. I merely observe.

STUART: Too modest. You're an example to us all.

ERIC: I like to think my mind was broad enough to change.

STUART: Don't we all. But, here I am, stuck in this straitjacket of ideals and ideology, of history and experience. I just can't seem to shake it off. If only I could be like you.

ERIC: Your cloth cap's showing, dear.

STUART: So's your fake suntan, but I'm too polite to mention that.

Pause.

ERIC: So what brings you to Paul Cash's office? Apart from the brandy?

STUART: Why, my undoubted talents as a film-maker, of course.

ERIC: Oh? Got the NUM account, has he?

STUART: You wouldn't be here if he had.

ERIC: That's true. I don't work for losers. (STUART *pours another drink.*) I feel like I'm being judged here.

STUART (*smirking*): Doesn't history judge us all?

ERIC: Oh God. One of the reasons I got out of the Labour Party was to escape from all that bloody council house, second-rate Leninist rhetoric. Or Dennis Skinner, as it's more commonly known. (STUART *laughs*.) Ah. You were being ironic.

STUART: It's a possibility.

CASH *and* ROBIN *come in, mid-discussion*:

ROBIN: . . . references, Paul. It's called visual wit. Remember?

CASH: It's too prissy. Too bloody fey. Minimum impact. I want the truth about the product. Hello, Eric. (*He pats him on the shoulder.*) We're not pouring cream on, we're getting the cream out.

ROBIN: But what's wrong with moving onto a larger canvas?

CASH: Nothing, so long as it's not designed by another art school reject friend of yours.

ROBIN: Get 1987 for Christ's sake, Boss.

CASH: Rob . . . try again. Dump the artwork. Keep the text if you must. But give me a wonderful experience. Please. (ROBIN *throws his hands in the air.*) And do it now. Sit this one out? (ROBIN *stares at him.*) We'll bring you in when we've got some basics worked out. OK?

ROBIN *stands a second then goes out.* CASH *presses the intercom buzzer.*

Liz, no calls. (*He pours a coffee.*) Jesus, I want something bold and vivid to pass on to the agency, and he's giving me the history of art. (*He sits.*) OK. You two met?

ERIC: We're old friends.

CASH: Yeah? Good. Sit down, Stuart. Come on, let's get formal. Right. Eric, did you tell Stuart where we are on this?

STUART: Apparently we're all in love with the Tory Party.

CASH: Yeah, that's right. For the purposes of this campaign, we are.

STUART: This is all a bit sudden.

CASH: Last month I was heavily involved with British Airways. Next month I fully intend to be having a torrid affair with the South African Tourist Board.

STUART: You really put it about.

CASH: That's the nature of the beast.

STUART: Mind you don't catch something.

CASH: I've had the jabs. I'm germ free. (*Beat.*) Are you familiar with Eric's column, Stuart?

STUART: Is that the one in Trafalgar Square. . .? (ERIC *chuckles.*)

CASH: Don't fuck about, man.

STUART: Well, if you ask me questions like that, it could very quickly be the end of a beautiful relationship.

CASH: Come on. Have you read it?

STUART: Yes.

CASH: And? (*Beat.*)

STUART: Forgive me, but, it's smug, self-satisfied, lowest common denominator crap. (ERIC *chuckles.*) The guy's in love with the starch of Margaret Thatcher's skirts. (*Beat.*) He despises the working class, because that's where he comes from. He's dangerously nostalgic, a cynic masquerading as a realist. In short, his bank roll's so far down his throat, it's coming out his arse. Oh, and he probably wants to travel and help children. (*Beat*) Can I go now? (ERIC *laughs.*)

ERIC: It's true! That's what they say. Grown men and women turn into little play-ground bullies. It's pathetic. We can nail this in the film, Paul. They don't want a Labour government, they want to take their bat and ball home so people like us won't be allowed to play any more. (*Beat. He's enjoying himself.*) Stuart, have you ever been to Party conference?

STUART: Once.

ERIC: Let me tell you . . . the bit I hate most. It's those beady-eyed little fanatics with the badges and the look of the converted. Staring at each other in corners, repeating their mantra:

'Jobs and services, welfare state, jobs and services.' I used to stand there thinking: my dad was a metalworker, you pasty-faced little white-collar shits. He held my hand on the terraces at Old Trafford. He was a shop steward, a full-time union official when there was still somethng to fight for. And if one of you disordered little twerps had ever dared call him comrade, he'd have wrung your bloody neck.

STUART: So much for the brotherhood of man.

ERIC: Sexist.

STUART: The only time I went, I can't say as I was as revolted by the rank and file as you obviously were. No, it was the PLP who got up my nose. The sleek patricians of Westminster, with their directorships, their consultancies, their newspaper columns. You lot went into a room, and by the time you came out, something was decided. Because that's how it worked. The poor silly ordinary bastards worked like slaves to get you elected, and from then on you made the decisions. As if it was God's law. Well, I had a good chuckle watching those jaws drop when they realised they were going to have to stand for reselection. Like someone had just told them the earth was flat.

ERIC: Reselection, yes. The revenge of the pygmies. (*Pause.*)

CASH: Well. Old wounds don't heal, do they?

ERIC: Not the oldest wound of all, the Labour Party. It still gushes blood, the poor old thing.

CASH: The point is, Stuart, that your attitudes are no longer those of the ordinary Labour voter. You represent, shall I say, a hard rump.

ERIC: No, don't mention Eric Heffer.

STUART: Christ.

CASH: Britain has changed, shifting class barriers, new technology, the Alliance . . .

STUART: Spare me the Murdoch memorial lecture.

CASH: I know you don't want to hear it but it's where we have to start from.

Now somewhere in there is a mainstream critique of Tory policy. I want us to identify it, agree on it and counter it.

STUART: Isn't that Bright's job?

ERIC: Don't look at me. I'm in love with the starch of Margaret Thatcher's skirts.

CASH: Don't be shy, Stuart. Put the emotion on hold and let's have the intellect in functioning mode for a change. What are the Tories' main weaknesses?

STUART: How long have you got?

CASH: As long as it takes.

ERIC: It *is* important to agree, if we're going to get into bed together on this one.

STUART: I'll keep my trousers on if it's all right with you.

ERIC: Oh dear. We shouldn't really be part of the same country, should we?

STUART: We're not.

ERIC: 'Twas ever thus. (*Beat.*)

CASH: Finished? (*Beat.*)

STUART: OK. Thatcher broke the unions to create a docile workforce, to get people back into a mobile labour market, a commodity, stripped of rights and representation. Also to push down real wages so the new industries could be manned at cheaper rates, making them economically viable for the immediate future. She financed unemployment with the money from North Sea oil, and floated a boom which let international capital alter the structure of British industry to such an extent that it would be impossible to reform it back again. How's that for an obituary?

ERIC (*making notes*): Right. Economic argument. Piece of cake.

STUART: The Welfare State has to be dismantled, sorry, rationalised, because it's an example of collective security, altruism if you like, which uses money, but, horror of horrors, doesn't make anybody a profit. Cannot make anybody a profit. So, smash it up. Private medicine makes a profit. Taxed benefits get something back at least. Stands to reason, push more and more people into private health care by making the NHS so piss-poor that only the dregs will still be able to bear to use it. For the dregs, read whole areas of previously employed Britain, now reduced to industrial rubble. Like the northeast.

ERIC (*writing*): Tory health cuts myth! (*Beat.*)

STUART: Down in Lambeth there's a derelict site, one of many, where young Londoners, black and white, dressed as New York hoodlums, chased Charles Bronson around for a couple of weeks while the cameras rolled. (*Beat.*) Where this recreation of Yankee social blight was being filmed, had once been a hospital. They knocked down a hospital and made *Death Wish Three* on the ruins.

ERIC: Anti-Americanism. Good. (*Beat.*)

STUART: Is there anybody out there?

CASH: You bet.

ERIC: That's really smashing, Stuart. (STUART *goes to the kitchen and pours a brandy.*) We've got the right man here all right, Paul.

HOWARD *and* GILL *have come into reception.*

STUART: Were you born a prat, Bright, or do you practise?

CASH: Hey, this is work, Clarkie.

ERIC: Politics, not personalities. Right, Mr Clarke?

LIZ *shows* HOWARD *and* GILL *into the office.*

CASH: Howard.

HOWARD: Cash. (ERIC *stands, rather sycophantically and holds out his hand.*) Bright.

ERIC: Hullo.

HOWARD: Still on our side, are you?

ERIC: Oh, yes.

HOWARD *licks his finger and holds it up to test the wind direction.*

HOWARD: Yes. Still blowing our way, I think. Cash, meet Gillian Huntley.

CASH: Hello. (*They shake hands.*)

HOWARD: Gill's taking over from Ronnie Whistler up in Lincoln come the next big one.

CASH: Really? You're on the short list?

GILL: I've been selected, actually. (*beat.*)

CASH: Ah. Congratulations.

HOWARD: Still got a lot to learn though. Can we pencil in a day next week for a mock interview?

CASH: Oh, sure.

GILL: I've heard a lot about your expertise, Mr Cash.

CASH: Good, I hope.

GILL: Felicity Hammond sings your praises.

CASH: Ah yes. We were very successful there.

GILL: She won the seat.

CASH: And so will you.

HOWARD: Another one in the House. What's the world coming to, eh?

ERIC: Well, you have an excellent example to follow, my dear.

HOWARD: You surely don't mean me.

ERIC: I mean the PM.

GILL: I think she's an example to us all. Including the men.

ERIC: Especially the men.

HOWARD: Hmm. You're right of course. But I draw the line at twinset and pearls. (*Half-hearted laughter.*) Who's the wallah burglarising your best Napoleon, Cash?

CASH: Stuart, come and meet Howard. (STUART *ambles down.*)

HOWARD: Come on down, Stuart.

STUART: Why not? The price is right. (*He arrives.*)

CASH: Howard, meet Stuart Clarke. Film director extraordinaire.

They shake.

HOWARD: Stuart Clarke? Stuart Clarke?

STUART: Well, it was fun while it lasted.

HOWARD: No, no, old man. Great fan of yours. And the good lady wife. Well, her especially.

STUART: Don't tell me you've seen my films.

HOWARD: Of course.

STUART: And you like them?

HOWARD: Like them? We had money in two of them. (*Beat.*) Bloody good stuff. Politics daft as a brush, but what the hell, it's a free country. Made us a few shillings if I remember. In fact, I think I'm right in saying, your film, what was it . . . something with 'Life' in the title . . .

STUART: *A Backstreet Life.*

HOWARD: That's right. Well, *A Backstreet Life* bought us our villa in Greece.

STUART (*not unfriendly*): So that's where the money went.

HOWARD: 'Fraid so, yes. God, the wife will be so pleased. Listen, you must come to dinner. We'd be thrilled.

STUART: OK.

ERIC: I didn't know you were a patron of the arts, Howard.

HOWARD: No? Well write it down for future reference. Look, can't really stop, Cash. Just wanted to meet the team. Talking of which, where's our dusky chum?

CASH: Shall I get him?

HOWARD: God, no. He makes me nervous. (*Beat.*)

CASH: Can I get you anything? Coffee?

HOWARD: Yes. Gill, you'll do that for me, won't you? It's up there in the little pot. Thanks. (*She goes to pour the coffee.*) OK. Those of you who haven't been down a dark hole for the last few years will be aware that the Conservative Party consists, crudely but accurately, of two factions. Known as the Wets and the Dries. Or Gentlemen and Players as I prefer it.

GILL: Milk?

HOWARD: What? Yes. You will also be aware –

GILL: Sugar?

HOWARD: No thank you. Also be aware that I'm not especially aligned with either party. Which is to say that I once served Heath loyally and prayed to Keynes every night, and I now serve Thatcher loyally. No prayers, you will observe, in conviction politics. (GILL *gives him his coffee.*) Thank you. Now, there has emerged, recently, a grouping which wishes to steer a middle course between these two opposites, wet and dry. We, they, see it as vital that we present a package to the electorate which stresses the strengths of the Party as a whole. The Prime Minister obviously has great appeal for many people, but it is important that we don't allow our ability in depth to be swamped by just the one personality. So, some of us on the presentational side of things are keen to come up with a few examples of balanced, but effective, publicity. Not, I might say, without some opposition from both sides. I fear without it, we may lose the next general election. And HMS *Britannia* will be steering a course for the nearest bloody great iceberg. (*Beat.*)

STUART: Sort of a 'Did Six Million Really Die' exercise.

HOWARD: In a way.

STUART: Were Four Million Really Unemployed?

HOWARD: Not on our bloody figures they weren't! (*He laughs.*) Cash, you know the form. Get me something good.

CASH: Commitment to excellence. That's our promise, Howard.

HOWARD: Good. (*Beat.*) Well, we must be off. I've promised this young lady lunch somewhere she can throw bread rolls at Roy Hattersley. Adios.

They all say goodbye etc. HOWARD *and* GILL *go.*

STUART: So. It's not even the Tory Party we're working for here. It's the Eton and Harrow Tendency. (*He laughs.*)

ERIC: In my experience, you throw a

bread roll at Hattersley, he just eats it. (*Beat.*)

CASH: Howard's a smoothie, but I've worked with him for a couple of years now. I trust him. This could do us a lot of favours.

ERIC: I'm with you all the way.

STUART: Is that an election pledge? Because your track record's not overly impressive on that score.

ERIC: This is the *real* world, Mr Clarke. (*Beat.*)

CASH: Last time of asking, Stuart. No going back. Are you in?

STUART: In? I wouldn't miss it for the world. (*Beat.*)

CASH: I'll have Liz draw up a contract.

AMANDA *comes into reception.*

ERIC: Time I was off. Mr Murdoch wants three thousand words on popular capitalism by Thursday. Can't disappoint him. When shall we three meet again?

CASH: I'll call you. See if you can draft out a few ideas for next time.

ERIC: No problem. Oh, don't forget I've got a week's freebie in Montserrat coming up.

CASH: It's in the diary.

AMANDA *comes in.* LIZ *is behind her, but she gives up and goes back to her desk.* AMANDA *sees* STUART *and is taken aback.*

ERIC: Goodbye, then. (*He goes.*)

STUART: What are you doing here?

AMANDA: Come to take my husband to lunch, what else? Assuming there's maybe something to celebrate.

CASH: I'm just waiting on his references. Amanda, how are you? Long time no see. (*They kiss formally.*)

AMANDA: You haven't changed much since I last saw you.

CASH: Some things never change.

STUART: I've *had* lunch.

AMANDA: Liquid by the look of it.

STUART: Salad. We can go to a boozer. I'll just take a leak. (*He goes.*)

AMANDA: I thought he'd be gone by now, sorry.

CASH: You mean you came to see me?

AMANDA: Of course. I'm not the Sally Army. I don't follow him around like a soup kitchen. I gave that up years ago.

CASH: It's a bit risky. I'm going to be seeing rather a lot of your husband.

AMANDA: Good. That means you can see more of me. (*Pause.*) Sod this. I want to kiss you. On the mouth. I want to lick your tongue.

CASH: I'd like that.

AMANDA: You like everything. You're undiscriminating.

CASH: It's this lust for life. I can't help it. (*Beat.*)

AMANDA: What about this evening?

CASH: What about it?

AMANDA: Are you free?

CASH: I could be.

AMANDA: Don't fuck me about Paul. You're not so hard to get.

CASH: Ring me after lunch. (*Beat.*) I may be busy.

AMANDA: I could come late. Do it on your desk. Mess up your papers.

CASH: How come we never do it on your desk?

AMANDA: Open plan office, darling. I may be many things, but an exhibitionist isn't one of them. Some things I keep to myself.

STUART *comes back in.*

STUART: Right.

AMANDA: Did you wash your hands?

STUART: Shove it.

AMANDA: Anybody'd think you just *lost* a job.

STUART: I just lost *some*thing. Fuck knows what. (*Beat.*) Come on. (*They turn to go.*) Propaganda, Cash. That's what you said.

CASH: That's right.

STUART: Pretty pictures. You're on.

STUART *and* AMANDA *go.* CASH

sits at his desk. LIZ *comes in.*

LIZ: D'you want some lunch?

CASH: No thanks. (*Beat.*)

LIZ: I like him.

CASH: Stuart?

LIZ: Aye.

CASH: He's an easy guy to like. Or he used to be. (*Beat.*) He was nearly killed, you know. In Ulster.

LIZ: I didn't know.

CASH: Yeah. (*He starts to smile.*) He was going to make a film. Pro IRA. Silly sod got caught in one of their city centre bombings. Complete accident. (*He laughs.*) Sorry. But you've got to laugh.

She stands for a second then picks up some papers from his desk.

LIZ: Are these signed?

CASH: Yeah.

She goes. CASH *smiles to himself.*

Blackout.

Scene Four

About ten o'clock that night. The office is quite dark. CASH *is stretched out on the sofa. After a moment's pause, a young man,* DOOLEY, *comes in. He's drying his hands on a paper towel. He crosses the room and throws the towel into the waste bin.*

DOOLEY: So. Paul. Are you often to be found in the Moulin Cinema Complex, Great Windmill Street? (*Beat.*) Are you?

CASH: Occasionally. (*Beat.*)

DOOLEY: Tell me, was it *Ranch of the Nymphomaniac* or possibly *Erotic Exploits of a Sexy Seducer* which drew you to this place? Or were you merely in out of the cold?

CASH: It's a warm night. (*Beat.*) *Prisoner of Paradise* was the film that particularly caught my eye.

DOOLEY: The overtones of confinement, was it? You were expecting perhaps, bondage or some such? (*Beat.*) You should see the one with the Queen in it. *Detained at Her Majesty's Pleasure.* (Beat.) I'll have that drink now.

CASH: Help yourself. It's in the fridge.

DOOLEY: One for yourself?

CASH: I'll have a Scotch.

DOOLEY: I hate the stuff. (*He takes a beer out of the fridge and pours a Scotch.*) Y'know, people say it's Scotch whisky that makes the Scots the way they are. Well I'm the way I am and I hate the stuff. (*Beat.*) Personally, I find the deletion of the erect male organ a great disappointment, don't you? (*He hands* CASH *his drink*) In the films. I mean, we get to see every nook and cranny of the girls. The camera would appear to be fearless in its probing of the female extremities. But where are the throbbing willies? I sometimes feel like shouting out: where are the cocks?! Y'know?

CASH: You'd get thrown out.

DOOLEY: What, by those wee Pakistani fellers?

CASH: They carry knives. (*Beat.*)

DOOLEY: Maybe that's where all the cocks have gone, eh? The Pakistani fellers slice them off and put them into samosas.

CASH: Maybe.

DOOLEY: Nah. It's a wee little Englishman somewhere who decreed that we were not to be allowed sight of the aroused male member. Has to be. It's so typically fucking English, that. (*Pause.*) I like cocks.

CASH: You've told me.

DOOLEY: Did you decorate this place yourself? Nah, course you didn't. I expect you had a firm of interior designers do it all for you.

CASH: That's right.

DOOLEY: I knew it. And d'you know how I knew it? It's like a public lavvy in here. That's how I knew it. (*Beat.*) A very nice public lavvy, but all the same . . . Do you ever go home?

CASH: Not very often. I don't like going outside very much.

DOOLEY: That's why you favour the erotic cinema, I suppose.

CASH: No. (*Beat.*)

DOOLEY: It's weird, is it not? That you never go home, though you have one, and I'm sure it's very nice, not like a public lavvy at all, and I don't have a home but would very much like to go there. If I had one. Is that not weird? That definitely says something to me.

CASH: What?

DOOLEY: Hey, I'm no philosopher. Which is just as well. Can you see a Bertrand Russell sleeping in a cardboard box under the arches? No, you cannot.

CASH: Why not? George Orwell did it.

DOOLEY: Who?

CASH: Orwell. Wrote *1984*.

DOOLEY: Aye? Shite film. Fucking depressing. The music was OK. I like the Eurythmics. That Annie Lennox, she's worth a poke, eh? (*Beat.*) You've not got a clue who I'm talking about, have you?

CASH: I have the Eurythmics on compact disc, as a matter of fact.

DOOLEY: What, in your cheesy home you never go to?

CASH: That's right.

DOOLEY: Maybe I should burgle you. Steal Annie Lennox off you.

CASH: Be my guest. I'm insured. (*Beat.*) Crap in the bed. Whatever it is you do. (*Beat.*)

DOOLEY: You really wouldn't mind?

CASH: Not in the slightest.

DOOLEY: Don't you want all the things you own?

CASH: I don't know what I want. All I know is, what I get isn't enough. (*Beat.*) What do *you* want?

DOOLEY: Me? Fucking everything. I want a house, a couple of cars, flash, with stereo speakers and tinted windows. I want an American Express card. A video. Loads of coke. An Armani suit. And I wanna be on Wogan.

CASH (*genuine*): So? Do it.

DOOLEY: Oh, aye . . .

CASH: Why not? It's there. You can have it.

DOOLEY: Gonna give it to me, are you?

CASH: No, it's easier than that. You just walk in and take it. (*Beat.*) If you weren't so bloody terrified of success, you could have it.

DOOLEY: I'm not terrified of nothing.

CASH: Wise up. You're all the same. You hang around Piccadilly Circus all day because you want to. You enjoy sleeping in a box. It's easy. You know that to go out and get what you want means standing on your own two feet. And that's something you never learned. Well I'll tell you, it's easier than spending your life whining on about how you're never going to get it.

DOOLEY: If I get it, I'm depriving somebody else of it, am I not?

CASH: So?

DOOLEY: And you, at this very moment, are in fact depriving me of what is rightfully mine.

CASH: But I'm sharing it with you.

DOOLEY: Not sharing. Bartering. I'm allowed to dip my wee toe into your pool on the understanding that at some point I may agree to play with your erect member. Or allow you to play with mine. Or put it in my mouth. Or worse. (*Beat.*) You've bought me. Is that not right?

CASH: In a sense. But in a sense, we're all bought and sold.

DOOLEY: Aye. Except how come when *I'm* bought and sold I feel like a Filipino or a twelve-year-old Bangkok virgin?

CASH: That's your speciality. That's your area. (*Beat.*) Anyway, who said anything about sex? (*Pause.*)

DOOLEY: I'll help myself.

He goes to the kitchen and gets another beer.

Like I said. I like cocks. (*He smiles, thinking he may have gone too far.*)

CASH: Do you have many friends?

DOOLEY: No. Do you?

CASH (*Beat*): No. I don't.

DOOLEY: Is that why you're talking to me?

CASH: No. (*Beat.*)

DOOLEY: What's your speciality, Paul? What's your area?

CASH: I tell lies for a living.

DOOLEY: Are you good at it?

CASH: One of the best. It's a very crowded market these days, but I like to think I've carved out my own little niche.

DOOLEY: Who do you tell these lies for?

CASH: Whoever pays me.

DOOLEY: And who do you tell them *to*?

CASH: Everybody. You. All the people who can't afford to pay me.

DOOLEY: Have you been telling me lies tonight?

CASH: Who knows? (*Beat.*) Why have you been following me? Why did you leave threatening phone calls on my answering machine? (*Beat.*)

DOOLEY: You must have somebody else in mind. I never met you before tonight. Halfway through *Warm Nights, Hot Pleasures* at the Moulin Cinema. The bit where the young girl found herself alone in the kitchen with the chauffeur and the gardener. (*Beat.*) And then the governess came in.

CASH: Why?

DOOLEY: I believe she was interested in some form of perverted sex. I missed the crucial next section as you engaged me in conversation. Something to do with how much of the film had you already missed. Lucky, really, that you didn't turn up ten minutes earlier. Ten minutes earlier I had my hand in the pocket of a middle-aged gentleman, performing executive relief for the price of the cinema ticket. If you were after more of the same, I was going to have to ask you to change sides as my left wrist was flagging just a wee bit.

The right's much stronger. Practice, y'see.

The doorbell in reception suddenly rings. They freeze. It rings again, more insistent. CASH gets up and goes to the window. He looks down.

CASH: Shit. You have to go.

DOOLEY: Now?

CASH: Yes. (*He ushers him to the door.*) Go into the office on the right, and as soon as it's clear, get down the stairs and let yourself out. I'll meet you tomorrow. Same place. OK? (*Beat.*)

DOOLEY: OK.

The doorbell rings again. DOOLEY goes out. CASH goes to the intercom and speaks into it.

CASH: Look, why don't you kids piss off. This is the last time . . .

AMANDA: Paul? It's me, Amanda.

CASH: Oh, Christ, sorry darling. I thought it was the bloody kids again. Hang on. I'll let you in.

He presses the buzzer and goes to the office and arranges his desk to make it look as if he's been working. Then he sits and picks up a pen. He notices an empty beer can, gets up and puts it in the bin. He sits again. After a moment, AMANDA comes in with a bottle of wine.

AMANDA: Help me drink this. Please. (*He gets up and kisses her and takes the bottle and goes to uncork it.*) Guess why Maxwell's back in town early. (*Beat.*)

CASH: You're sacked?

AMANDA: No. Reorganisation.

CASH: Sacked sideways.

AMANDA: Not even that. Sacked upwards. (*Beat.*) My salary's been raised by four thousand, my department's been enlarged, and I feel like I've been sacked. (*Beat.*) Of course, I've got a couple of placements in the department that weren't exactly my idea. Daughters of friends, that sort of thing. But, what the hell? I can cope. Nevertheless, there's a nasty smell of nepotism in the air. Also, a smell of impending reshuffle. (*Beat.*)

Paris was mentioned. And New York.

CASH: I see.

AMANDA: It's been mentioned before. Nothing ever came of it.

CASH: Sounds like you're being given a trial.

AMANDA: It does, doesn't it?

CASH: Is it what you want?

AMANDA: Yes. I suppose. (*Beat.*) At this rate, I'm never going to have kids.

CASH: I didn't think you wanted any.

AMANDA: I don't.

CASH: Well, then. (*She runs her fingers through his hair and kisses his face.*)

AMANDA: Mess up the papers?

CASH: Darling . . . I've got to work. I'm behind on McLeish and Harper. And Robin's been playing silly buggers with the artwork. If I don't get it sorted a.s.a.p. we'll lose it.

AMANDA: Uh huh.

CASH: I know it's a bastard, but what can I do?

AMANDA: I don't know. (*Beat.*) Shit, I'm miserable. (*Beat.*) Post-anxiety depression, most probably. What I need is to get zonked and roll in the hay.

CASH: I am sorry. (*She sits. He's not happy.*)

AMANDA: I think I'd prefer Paris to New York. The language is easier. (*He smiles.*) How was Stuart?

CASH: Oh, you know . . .

AMANDA: No . . .

CASH: He was a bit . . .

AMANDA: Prickly?

CASH: That I can handle. It's just a very funny situation. Me employing *him*.

AMANDA: Somebody's got to.

CASH: But he hates my guts. Always has done. (*Beat.*) Still, playtime's over. After all these years, Stuart's had to grow up.

AMANDA: You're enjoying it. (*Beat.*)

CASH: Yeah. I'm helping the guy out,

but . . . I guess revenge is sweet.

AMANDA: Very in tune with the times.

CASH: What is?

AMANDA: Oh, revenge. (*Beat.*) Anyway, I'm glad it worked out. I've been on at him for months. In fact, I think *he* sees it as getting revenge. He likes to think you can't live without him. We both know you can, but you boys, you have to have your illusions.

CASH: Why so keen to get us together?

AMANDA: Christ, Paul, haven't you ever heard of symmetry? (*Beat.*)

CASH: You don't, by any chance, want to have your cake and eat it?

AMANDA: Don't be silly.

CASH: Or maybe it's a way of softening the blow.

AMANDA: What blow?

CASH: Letting one of us down easily. (*Beat.*)

AMANDA: I love you, Paul.

CASH: And you love Stuart.

AMANDA: Not in the same way.

CASH: How many different ways are there?

AMANDA: Hundreds. Look, don't get jealous, for Christ's sake. (*Beat.*) What am I saying? I'm telling my lover not to be jealous of my husband. Something's wrong here. (*Beat.*) Stuart and I have been together for a long time. We gave up bothering to love each other properly years ago. But I love you. (*Beat.*) We'll never have the same sort of relationship as I had with Stuart. I mean, I think once in a lifetime is enough for all that stuff. In fact, I don't think I'm capable of it any more. I'm too proud now to become a couple again.

CASH: So, basically, I'm your little bit on the side.

AMANDA: I like the sound of that. (*Beat.*) It's all there is. Take it or leave it.

CASH: I'll leave it for tonight, if that's OK with you.

AMANDA: Sure. (*Beat.*) Paul, when I

say I love you, that's what I mean. I don't mean I want to marry you and have your children and go all starry-eyed when you walk in the room and sing your praises to your boss and . . . *look after you.* I want someone to do that for me. And if they can't, then the occasional bout of lovemaking will do just as nicely thank you. I've got a job and a life to look out for. And it's a dirty job, but somebody's got to do it, and if it isn't me, then it's not going to be any other bugger.

CASH: Yeah. (*Beat.*) I should have made my pitch for you nearly twenty years ago.

AMANDA: No way. You were foul. Then. (*The phone rings.*)

CASH: It's OK. It's on the answering machine.

The machine clicks on. LIZ*'s voice speaks.*

LIZ: Hello, Cash Creative Consultancy. (CASH *pours a Scotch.*) I'm sorry, there's nobody in the office at the moment to take your call, but if you'd like to leave your name and number, we'll get back to you as soon as possible. Please speak after the tone. Thank you for calling.

The tone sounds. It is STUART.

STUART: Hi, Cash, uh, Paul . . . yeah, it's Stuart. (CASH *and* AMANDA *look at each other.*) Look, I just wanted to say . . . thanks. I hope I wasn't too much of an arsehole today . . . I'm a bit out of practice, that's all. (*Beat.*) I've started doing some research. Got some good ideas. If you want to give me a ring, I'll go over them with you. (*Beat.*) Hey, don't worry about Bright. He's a spiv. I know all about them. (*Beat.*) It'll be great to get behind a camera again. There's a lot of things I'm learning to do again. (*Beat.*) Listen mate, strictly between us . . . I made love to Amanda for the first time in months this morning. After you called. You're obviously a bigger turn on than we ever thought, Cash. (AMANDA *closes her eyes.*) Anyway . . . it's, uh, good to be on board. Yours for a great

Conservative campaign and a Labour victory. Bye.

The line goes off. Pause.

AMANDA: Don't you dare give me a hard time for sleeping with my husband. (*Beat.*)

CASH: I really have to get on with this. (*Beat.*)

AMANDA: Yeah. (*She stands and stares at him.*) Yeah.

She picks up her bag and goes. CASH *stands, hands in pockets, for a second, then takes off his tie and begins to undress, slowly, methodically, deep in thought. Finally, naked, he sits at his desk and finishes his Scotch.* DOOLEY *comes back in.*

DOOLEY: But, as I soon became aware . . . (CASH *starts.*) . . . you weren't in the market for executive relief of the kind only I can give in the stalls of the Moulin cinema. So you engaged me in idle chat and I thought to myself, this wee man's just a wee bit lonely. Company. That's all he's after. Am I right? (*Beat.*) I didnae leave, as you can see. I'll go if you want.

CASH: No. That's all right.

DOOLEY: I was browsing through your man's desk in there . . . (*He paces around, taking off his clothes as he goes.*) . . . and I was taking a look at some of the crap he had in there. Heavy. Intellectual stuff, no doubt. But surely you don't have to have a degree to lie to people. Maybe it helps, I dunno. But low, animal cunning must play a large part in this charade. And I am blessed with that particular commodity by the bucketful. I have a very resourceful nature. So.

He stands, naked, by CASH. *After a pause,* CASH *stands.*

I want to be employed. (*Beat.*)

CASH: I want to be loved.

Beat, then CASH*'s hand goes out to* DOOLEY.

Blackout.

22 FASHION

ACT TWO

Scene One

Mid-morning a week later. CASH is in the kitchen, leaning against the table drinking a cup of coffee. ROBIN is in the office setting up the video camera tripod. LIZ enters with some papers and goes to the desk.

CASH: Is that the Benson stuff?

LIZ: And the Windfall contracts.

CASH: Good. Liz, see if you can raise Billy at Machin & Drew for me, will you? If he's in court, leave a message. Say it's the Benson file.

LIZ: Uh huh. (*She goes.*)

ROBIN: Windfall's definitely going through then, is it?

CASH: You bet. They're convinced they can get a bigger share of mind now we've shown them how to unlock the strengths of the product.

ROBIN: A two-year-old could have done that.

CASH: But a two-year-old didn't. We did. Actually, I hate to say it, but your idea of putting them with Ronnie at the Tate agency was brilliant. Sticking with Todd's was flogging a dead horse. I'm eternally grateful.

ROBIN: So give me a rise.

CASH: See my lawyer.

DOOLEY comes in with a portable video camera. He now wears a smart suit, shirt, and has a trendy haircut. He takes the camera to the tripod.

DOOLEY: This is a real beauty. Light as a feather. Feel that. Weighs nothing at all.

ROBIN: I know. (*They start setting it up.*)

DOOLEY: I wouldn't mind one of these for Christmas. Hire myself out for weddings and that. Bar mitzvahs. Orgies. Make a fortune. That's how Spielberg started, y'know. Aye. I was talking to a guy in a pub, from one of the film companies in Wardour Street, and he said that Steven Spielberg

started with home movies.

ROBIN: Fascinating.

DOOLEY: That's what I thought.

CASH has come down and is looking through the papers on his desk.

CASH: You can set this up, can't you?

ROBIN: Yeah.

CASH goes out to talk to LIZ.

DOOLEY: What's all this in aid of, then?

ROBIN: If you were meant to know, somebody would have told you.

DOOLEY: Well, I'm asking you. (*Beat.*) Is it your toy? Is that it? (*Beat.*) Well, the whole fucking place can't be your toy, now can it? (*Beat.*) Say something, even if it's only fuck off.

ROBIN: Fuck off.

DOOLEY *laughs.*

DOOLEY: You're fulla crap, you know that?

ROBIN: Oh, just shut up and get on with it.

DOOLEY *lights a cigarette.*

DOOLEY: Pardon me for breathing, pal. Excuse me for polluting your air space. But I work here, much as you dislike it, I know. I am on the payroll. On the books. Official. So don't give me a hard time.

ROBIN: Look, I know why you're here. I don't like it, but there you are.

DOOLEY: You're breaking my heart.

ROBIN: I know you're just a ponce. You'll be gone soon. To ponce off someone else. So it's no skin off my nose. Just don't get in my way, that's all.

Beat, then DOOLEY grabs him by the collar.

DOOLEY: You smooth little bastard. Does it get that far up your nose, eh? Seeing someone like me in your place? (*He lets go.*)

ROBIN: Just move on somewhere else.

DOOLEY: I'm staying, pal. It's you who'll have to do the moving.

ROBIN: I know it may be quite an effort, but think for a minute. I've been here nearly two years. I know this business. I'm qualified. I'm fucking good. You've been here a week. You're a gofer. A nobody. You don't know the business. You don't know shit. (*Beat.*) Now, the first sign of unpleasantness, who do you think abandons ship? Got it? You. You're trash. The suit doesn't hide that. Pal.

STUART *comes in to look through the videos.*

STUART: Ay ay, what's this?

ROBIN: Interview drill. Cash teaches the candidates not to pick their noses on *Panorama.*

STUART: Really?

ROBIN: Really.

STUART *has the video he was looking for.*

CASH *comes back in.*

CASH: Cut the chat, boys. Let's see some work around here.

DOOLEY: Sorry, Mr Cash.

He goes out to reception where LIZ *gives him an envelope which he goes out with.*

STUART: Hey, Cash, I think I've come up with a slogan.

CASH: Hit me.

STUART: 'Nobody with a conscience ever votes Conservative.'

CASH: Snappy. But stick to the pictures.

STUART: Whatever you say. (*He goes out.*)

CASH: Rob?

ROBIN: What?

CASH: Come on. Meditate on your own time. Is that thing ready to go?

ROBIN: Yeah. (*Beat.*) I think we should talk.

CASH: About what?

ROBIN: About the company. About Young Lochinvar.

CASH: Ho ho. How long did it take you to think that one up?

ROBIN: Get smart, boss. He's a user.

CASH: So am I. So, for that matter, are you. It's good for business.

ROBIN: He could be very bad for business. Unless you want to be known as Rent Boy Limited.

CASH: OK, shut up.

ROBIN: No. And what's more, when do we get round to discussing making me a partner? It *was* part of the deal. (*Beat.*)

CASH: First, I didn't notice anybody making any derogatory comments when I took you on –

ROBIN: Well, Christ, at least I've had some formal education –

CASH: Oh pardon me. Private school and Polytechnic of North London. I forgot you were so well connected.

ROBIN: I mean, at least I have some qualification for the work.

CASH: He's got the best qualification you can get. He wants it. I can turn him into anything. You'll always be an arty bastard, good for some things, but dodgy on the big stuff. You'll make a great living, no doubt about that, but you'll never take the world by the throat.

ROBIN: And he will?

CASH: No, I will. But he'll be there. (*Beat.*) And I'll think about making you a partner when you straighten out McLeish and Harper.

ROBIN: What's wrong with it now, for Christ's sake?

CASH: Nothing much. It could be better, that's all. Show it to Dooley. See what he thinks.

ROBIN: You are joking, of course.

CASH: No. (*Pause.*)

ROBIN: OK, Paul, you've made your point. I'm sorry. Ideas above my station, etcetera. But please . . . ditch the rough trade. It's you I'm thinking of.

CASH: I'm touched. (*Beat.*) If you weren't so precious, you'd understand. He's useful. To that boy, nothing is sacred. That's what I want. So for now,

I'll let him run errands, hang around, upset you, I'll pay him, because one day, I'll open the box and there he'll be, fully formed. Ready to be unleashed on an unsuspecting world. And let's face it, the world saw *you* coming a mile off. We can't afford to stagnate, Robin, my old mate.

HOWARD *comes into reception.*

ROBIN: You're going to fall flat on your face, you know.

CASH: I got here by taking risks, not by worrying about my image.

HOWARD *comes in.*

Howard, hello.

HOWARD: Morning. No sign of Miss Huntley?

CASH: Not yet.

HOWARD (*looking at his watch*): Good God. A fault. At last. I was beginning to think she could walk on water.

CASH: Think about what I said, Rob. OK?

ROBIN: Oh, yeah. Say goodbye, Rob. Goodbye, Rob.

He goes.

HOWARD: Is Bright in on this one?

CASH: Yes.

HOWARD: He's terribly good, isn't he? Terribly clever.

CASH: Yes.

HOWARD: I loathe him, though. Can't help it. Him and his kind, they're all the same. Stab their own in the back, then come over to us and start preaching the gospel. The fanaticism of the convert. (*Beat.*) Still, they're as nothing compared to this new breed of woman we keep getting. Clones of 'Herself'. Heads on one side, the voice of sweet reason, they're like a lot of little girls at a talent competition. All impersonating the same woman. One day, they'll be standing there in front of the voters, and suddenly the penny will drop. And the people will laugh. With every copied bloody mannerism the laughter will grow and grow until they all run from the podium screaming and crying, never to be seen again.

(*Beat.*) I've been shafting her, you know.

CASH: The Prime Minister?

HOWARD: No, bloody fool. The Huntley woman.

CASH: Oh.

HOWARD: Back to her hotel after lunch, you know . . .

CASH: Is this wise?

HOWARD: No, it bloody well isn't. Don't know what came over me. Just have to hope she was too pissed to remember. Hasn't mentioned it since. But she's been behaving . . . as if she has something on me.

CASH: Well she does. Not exactly in the job description, is it? I mean, candidate training doesn't usually involve sleeping with Party whips.

HOWARD: No, not since matron took over. (*Beat.*) God, why are we always sexually attracted to danger areas?

ERIC *has come into reception.*

CASH: I'll take a raincheck on that one, Howard.

ERIC *comes in.*

ERIC: Good morning.

CASH: Morning.

ERIC: Where's the suspect?

CASH: Not here yet.

ERIC: Black mark. Note that down, Howard.

CASH: Sorry, let me get you something to drink. (*He speaks into the intercom.*) Liz. Coffee, please.

ERIC: Had dinner with Paul Johnson last night. We're going to be working together on the box.

HOWARD: Crackerjack?

ERIC (*chuckling*): No, Howard. New discussion programme on Channel Four. Politics and morality. (*Beat.*)

HOWARD: Well. They certainly picked the right two there.

ERIC: Thank you.

LIZ *comes in and goes to get the coffee.*

CASH: It's good to see someone other

than redbrick Marxists talking politics on the box. It's about time the left orthodoxy was booted off our screens.

ERIC: Slow process, Paul. Slow process. But yes, it's happening.

HOWARD: I won't believe it until the BBC's cleaned up.

ERIC: Privatisation. It's got to come. Then they won't have a rock to hide under. Daft middle-class Oxbridge Trots. Let them try and make a living in the real world.

LIZ *puts a tray of coffee down and goes. They help themselves.*

HOWARD: Tell me, Bright –

ERIC: Call me Eric, Howard, everybody does.

HOWARD: Yes, Eric. How does it come about that someone with such an implacable hatred of all things middle-class finds himself on our side?

ERIC: Oh, Howard, didn't they tell you?

HOWARD: What?

ERIC: The Tory Party's gone populist. Surely you'd noticed.

HOWARD: But we haven't gone anti-middle-class.

ERIC: No, we're on the offensive against the trendy middle class. The left middle class. The ones who consider themselves the natural allies of the proletariat. Islington. Lambeth. The ones who want to nanny the working class. Who want them underprivileged. (*Beat.*) Unfortunately for them, whole swathes of working people vote Tory. You see them, horny-handed sons of toil with the *Sun* in their back pocket. Superhod. The brickie with the Roller. Holidays in Spain. Youth mobilised not against Fascism, youth mobilised for sangría and a suntan. And patriotism, that good old working-class virtue, is back in fashion. Pride. Self-reliance. Working-class virtues, Howard. Many years ago, I joined the Labour Party because I thought it was a radical party. But it's a sheep in wolf's clothing. Margaret Thatcher's Tory Party is the true radical force in this country today. That's why I support you. This government has delivered

what Labour promised. (*Beat.*)

HOWARD: This is all most disorientating.

ERIC: You don't have to apologise for being rich any more, Howard. It's a bright new day. (*Beat.*)

CASH: Shall we . . .?

ERIC: Sorry, I get rather carried away. Right, Paul.

CASH: How d'you want to run things, Howard?

HOWARD: Same as usual. We'll do the interview, you come up with any presentation stuff, Paul.

ERIC: Smashing.

HOWARD: Just one thing . . . she's going to be up against a pretty tough opponent in the election, majority's only a couple of thou, and the Alliance are threatening whatever it is they always threaten, so, let's not make it easy for her. OK?

GILL *comes into reception.*

The rougher the ride, the more she'll benefit. Try to pierce the exterior. I want to see if she'll crack.

LIZ *shows* GILL *in.*

GILL: I'm most terribly sorry. My taxi was late, and then we got caught up in a demonstration. Honestly, the sooner we clear the streets, the better, in my view.

CASH: Liz, another coffee.

LIZ *goes and gets a cup.*

GILL: It's monstrous that in a city as busy as London these people are allowed to march wherever the fancy takes them.

HOWARD: Not to worry, Gill. Have a coffee and relax for a minute. Do you know everyone?

GILL: Yes, Mr Cash, hello. And Mr Bright, of course, I know from his excellent television programme.

ERIC: You're too kind.

GILL: I always make sure the whole family are watching. We gather round the television set every Sunday morning, all together.

ERIC: You make me sound like the abdication speech.

GILL (*laughing humourlessly*): Really, Mr Bright, nothing so dreary. (LIZ *has poured her coffee.*) Thank you. That's very kind.

CASH: Would you like to sit down?

GILL: Thank you.

They sit. LIZ goes.

CASH: Now then –

STUART *suddenly comes in, reading from a notepad and talking at the same time.*

STUART: How about this one, Cash? 'Vote Tory, otherwise Norman Tebbit will . . . (*He sees them.*) . . . sexually assault . . . your family . . . pets.' (*Beat.*) No. Well. Maybe not.

He goes.

CASH: Sorry. (HOWARD *and* ERIC *are smiling.*) Howard's explained all this set up to you, has he?

GILL: Thoroughly.

CASH: Good. Have you ever performed in front of cameras before?

GILL: I was interviewed once. On a council matter.

CASH: So it's not a completely new experience?

GILL: Not completely.

CASH: Fine. Eric and Howard will be asking the questions. I'll be watching the screen. Afterwards we can watch the video and take you through the interview again. Possibly suggest one or two ways you can present yourself more positively. If that's the case.

GILL: I'm sure I'll be very rough.

CASH: It's much easier than you think. Right. Let's get started.

They all stand and CASH sits GILL on an uncomfortable chair in front of the camera. ERIC and HOWARD sit just out of shot. GILL's face is up on the screen.

GILL: Will questions be specific? Or . . .?

ERIC: I expect we'll roam around all over the place.

GILL: Jolly good.

HOWARD: For the purposes of the test, assume us both to be hostile.

GILL: I'm sorry?

HOWARD: *Newsnight.*

GILL: Got you.

CASH: All right, then. In your own time.

Long pause while ERIC and HOWARD take out sheets of prepared questions and flick through the pages. CASH settles down on the sofa with a pad and pencil, kicking off his shoes and watching the screen. GILL becomes uncomfortable. ERIC suddenly breaks the silence in best interviewer style.

ERIC: Gillian Huntley. Hello.

GILL: Hello.

ERIC: May I first broach the thorny subject of the economy?

GILL: Please.

ERIC: Very well. The government is committed in the life of this Parliament to introducing tax cuts, whether on the basic rate or simply for the better off, the chancellor has not yet made clear.

GILL: That is correct, yes.

ERIC: Now, what I would like to ask is: how is he going to pay for this? It has been suggested in some quarters, maliciously perhaps, that he will have to steal from the poor to give to the rich. That he will have to squeeze the Public Sector Borrowing Requirement, the PSBR, even more than he is already doing, in order that those in work, those with a high income, will be given a little more money in their pocket, which he then hopes they will invest, and in so doing, promote the revitalisation which he smilingly informs us is just around the corner. (*Beat.*) Miss Huntley.

GILL: I have to say, uh, that your original statement was, uh, incorrect . . .

ERIC: Which statement? That the Government is committed to tax cuts?

GILL: No . . .

ERIC: Because I want to be very clear on this.

GILL: No, the bit about . . . stealing from the rich – I mean the poor – to give to the rich. That's incorrect.

ERIC: I see.

GILL: Yes. It is quite incorrect to say that we . . .

HOWARD: No no no. Sorry to interrupt, Paul, Eric. Miss Huntley, when a questioner says something you know to be an untruth, you tell him so. What he said was not incorrect, it was wrong! Wrong! Plain and simple. Clear as a bell. Murder is wrong. Terrorism is wrong. Labour is wrong. Got me?

GILL: Yes. Yes.

HOWARD: All right. Sorry, Eric, do go on.

ERIC: So where is the money to come from? Will you cut benefits? Defence? What will you do?

GILL: Well, first of all, Mr Bright, let me say that the cut in income tax must, in my opinion, be in the basic rate paid by all wage earners. The individual earns his wage and is entitled to spend it how he sees fit. The State has no business telling the ordinary wage earner how he should spend his money. And as a Conservative, I strongly believe that a man's money belongs in his own pocket, where he can decide how best to use it for himself and his family.

HOWARD (*bored*): But where will the money come from to finance tax cuts?

GILL: Oh. Yes. From defence, yes. We're keeping defence spending down by insisting on value for money.

HOWARD: So you're going to run down Britain's defence capability, are you?

GILL: That's not what I said.

HOWARD: That's what it sounded like.

ERIC: Miss Huntley, if I may move on? I think you've made your position reasonably clear on that one. What about the public sector? What about the Welfare State? Mrs Thatcher told us the health service was safe in her hands. The health service tells us it's dying the death of a thousand cuts.

GILL: Well . . .

ERIC: If I may . . . the teachers tell us that they are at their most demoralised. Lack of basic facilities, books for heaven's sake, run-down classrooms, the list goes on. And then there is their pay grievance. Just two of the traditionally moderate professions alienated, it would seem, by the Government's antagonistic social policies.

GILL: But, as you know, the Government is in fact spending more money, in real terms, on the health service today than at any time since its inception.

ERIC: But, as we also know, that, surely, is inevitable, with an aging population, inflation in the cost of drugs for treatment and so on. The point being made by many moderate men and women throughout the land, however, is that government policy is starving the hospitals and the teaching hospitals of the funds they need simply to remain open and maintain existing services.

GILL: Wastage in the health service has become rife. Waste, Mr Bright, is the key word. Waste of money. Waste of resources. Certain services had become inefficient and overmanned, like much of British industry in public ownership. But we are making the health service more efficient by hiring out catering and cleaning services to private contractors who deliver the goods at a reasonable cost. Our policies boost private and public enterprise alike.

ERIC: All right. We won't get into the issue of just how efficient those private contractors have proved to be, instead, let me move on to the other area I mentioned: education. What can be done to revive the demoralised corpse of education in this country?

GILL: Well, you know, the teachers were being offered a very fair deal. The majority of teachers' unions accepted that, because what we were offering was a deal based on the need for teachers to accept that they also have responsibilities to the service in which they work. We want to introduce a system which will seek out those who are inefficient, those who abuse their position for political ends, those who are responsible for the breakdown of discipline in our schools. Those rules apply in any other job, and so should they apply in the teaching profession.

ERIC: But the teachers say that this is all a smokescreen, a decoy behind which you keep their salaries down.

GILL: I think anybody who has ever agonised over the plight of the young in our society will feel, as I do, that you cannot measure dedication in terms of financial reward. Goodness knows, we all want to respect and look up to our teachers, but, I ask you, how can we when they refuse to supervise dinner breaks, extra-curricular activities and so on, when they introduce the tactics of industrial anarchy into our classrooms?

ERIC: What about the principle involved? The opposition have criticised you on just those grounds, that you have created two nations, with one set of workers being asked to accept a fall in their living standards while another are allowed pay rises way above the level of inflation.

GILL: I don't think there's very much the opposition can teach us about principle, do you? After all, they left us with rising inflation, debts, an economy in which we payed ourselves too much while not producing enough. Do you remember the winter of discontent? I do. And I never want to see another winter like it. And we have not. Since this Government came to power, the realism of our objectives has ensured stability and growth.

HOWARD: Unless you happen to be unemployed.

GILL: We care passionately about the unemployed. We want to see Britain back at work. But we want to see real jobs, not feather-bedding and overmanning, practices which lead to disaster. Take the miners. They have realised now that the future of their industry lies in work, not in strikes, in hard work. There will have to be closures, naturally, because as pits become exhausted, so they have to close. That has always been accepted. The Labour Party closed more pits than this Government. The Labour Party closed many, many hospitals as well. But we are portrayed as wishing to close these ventures for no good reason. What nonsense. We are simply applying the harsh remedies demanded by a harsh world recession. (*Beat.*)

ERIC: Thank you. You've made yourself very clear. Now. The years of this Conservative Government have seen, have they not, a general rise in lawlessness, real and perceived, as well as a sense of disillusion and cynicism about society as a whole. There is a feeling, correct me if I'm wrong, that we are on the whole, a less happy nation. We allow the government to ride roughshod over ideals and freedoms which we previously took for granted. We even, in certain circumstances, allow our sovereignty to be put in doubt. I'm thinking of, for instance, the invasion of Grenada or the bombing of Tripoli.

GILL: May I answer that in two parts? First: disorder, lack of discipline, lack of respect for authority are all things engendered in the young by that generation which grew up without benefit of guiding moral principles. The youth of the 1960s were encouraged to rebel, to profane, for no other reason than to annoy. At the same time, they were indoctrinated with decadent and anti-establishment ideas. These people now produce our television programmes, our films, our plays. They teach in our schools, they run many of our councils. They write for left-wing magazines. They are people who try to use freedom to destroy freedom. They have encouraged the young, already under pressure from social circumstances bequeathed to us by successive Labour governments, under pressure from waves of immigration, to adopt the nihilistic pose so fashionable in the sorry sixties. Children are *encouraged* to worry about nuclear arms which have kept the peace in Europe for over forty years. They are positively encouraged to fear and worry about their future. And in so doing, they are made unreachable by reason and good common sense. They are no longer taught respect for private property. They are taught envy and greet. They are no longer taught to have pride in their country. Instead, they are given politically biased so-called accounts of our imperial past as if it is something to be ashamed of. They are taught 'peace studies'. Policemen are no longer allowed into our schools. But any crackpot black is invited, yes invited, to stir up racial hatred and hatred of authority. Is it any wonder then, that these children steal, rape, riot, even murder, since without the restraint of civilisation and authority, that is human nature? (*Pause.*) Second: America is our greatest ally. She has bases in this country because we want them here. They are part of NATO's defence of Europe. Now, those bases are not here for decoration. They are here to be used. When a madman like Gaddafi threatens the civilised world with terrorism, what are we to do? Are we to do what successive Labour administrations have done? Nothing, at best. At worst, actually talk to these murderers. Or are we to take action? As we proved in the Falkland Islands, when British territory is threatened, we retaliate. (*Beat.*) When our very own streets are not safe, think how dangerous is the world outside our borders. (*Pause.*)

ERIC. Thank you. Most comprehensive.

She relaxes as if the interview is over.

HOWARD: Miss Huntley. Just a couple of points.

She tenses again. HOWARD *is furious but in control.*

You're a librarian, I believe.

GILL: That's right.

HOWARD: And you live with your parents.

GILL: Yes.

HOWARD: You're engaged to be married.

GILL: I am.

HOWARD: What does your fiancé do for a living?

GILL: He's a farmer.

HOWARD: I see. (*Beat.*) And you were educated locally at a private school.

GILL: Yes.

HOWARD: And you studied English and Philosophy at St. Andrew's University. (*Beat.*) You don't come from a very heavily industrialised area, I think I'm right in saying.

GILL: No, it's very peaceful.

HOWARD: I'm sure. And you've never worked in industry, or business.

GILL: Neither has Neil Kinnock.

HOWARD: Quite. (*Beat.*) You see, I'm just a little puzzled as to where you get your certainty from. I mean, it all sounds very familiar, it has the ring of truth about it, but . . . how do you know? (*Beat.*)

GILL: I talk to people. I read. Books. Newspapers.

HOWARD: Yes, of course, but, forgive me, I detect a sense of something rather unpleasant in what you say.

GILL: The truth often hurts.

HOWARD: God yes, but I detect something other than the truth. I detect, pardon me for saying it, a fear, an underlying prejudice against your fellow Britons. Not to mention the rest of the unAmerican world.

GILL: If you mean I don't like socialists, you're quite right.

HOWARD: No, I don't mean that. After all, not all teachers can be socialists, or all doctors, or nurses, or hospital administrators, or even miners for that matter. No, I mean, speaking as a fellow Briton, I get the impression that you feel we're just not good enough. We fail to measure up to some abstract standard you have for . . . attitude, behaviour. We're just not good enough, and you're jolly well going to do something about it! (*He smiles.*)

GILL: I believe that is what politicians are for. (*Beat.*)

HOWARD: Forgive me, but that is the most preposterous, dangerous nonsense it has ever been my misfortune to hear.

ERIC *finds something fascinating to do in his case.* CASH *reclines with his eyes closed.*

I have been in politics all my adult life.

I have known people who came into politics to further their business careers, to boost their egos, to fill an otherwise dull life, to fulfil the family tradition. I have even known people come into politics because they believe they have something useful to offer the nation. But I have never known anybody come into politics because they despise their country and wish to exorcise their fear and loathing with a good dose of corrective medicine. That is not political drive. That is psychological disorder. (*Beat.*) Please don't make the mistake of thinking that we want an army of steel-jawed, flaxen-haired warriors against all things decadent. Our leader is a one-off. She can't go on for ever. She is useful in the short term for enabling us to do what we do best: running the capitalist economy. But in the long term, she is just another servant of the Party. (*Beat.*) I just don't think we need any more like you. (*Beat.*) I'm sorry, Miss Huntley, if one day you put your little foot outside mother and father's ivy-covered cottage and saw lots of frightening things. I'm sorry if you didn't understand what all those horrible big grown-ups were doing, in their factories, their offices, their pubs, their bedrooms. I'm sorry they called you nasty names and they have to pay for it. They swore and didn't go to church very often; they did things Mummy and Daddy said weren't very nice. (*Beat.*) But I've got news for you. They've been doing it since the dawn of creation, and they're going to go on doing it whether you stamp your little foot and tell them to stop it or not. (*Beat.*) It's not society that has the problem, Miss Huntley. It's not society that's deviant. It's you. (*Beat.*) My advice would be to marry your farmer, produce your incredibly heavily EEC subsidised crops, have a couple of children, go to church regularly and quietly shrivel up in the peaceful English countryside. That, after all, is what it's there for.

STUART *puts his head round the door.*

STUART: What about: 'High fibre politics. Norman gets yer bowels moving'?

GILL *stands with a look of distress and betrayal and goes out.* STUART *watches her go.*

It wasn't that bad . . . (*He goes.*)

CASH: Well, Howard. (*Beat.*) You shouldn't have messed around like that. You should have really let her have it.

HOWARD: Cash, I've seen the future. And it freezes my water. (ERIC *chuckles.*) What?

ERIC: I was just thinking. You're in the wrong party, old fruit.

HOWARD: No. I'm not. She is.

ERIC *laughs.* HOWARD *joins in.*

CASH: Anybody need a drink?

HOWARD: Please. (CASH *goes to the kitchen.*) I'll tell you what.

CASH: What?

HOWARD: I don't know why I'm laughing.

CASH: No?

HOWARD: No. Because if Miss Huntley opens her mouth, I'm going to be up to my eyeballs in shit.

He roars with laughter. ERIC *laughs.* CASH *looks seriously at* HOWARD.

Blackout.

Scene Two

Later that day. Mid-afternoon. STUART *is alone in the office, watching a video of Grosvenor Square or demonstrations, making notes.* LIZ *comes in.*

LIZ: I'm sorry. Still no sign.

STUART: 'S OK, Liz.

LIZ: It's not like him. I mean, he doesn't even usually go out for lunch. A quick sandwich at his desk and that's it. I practically have to force-feed him.

STUART: You look after him, don't you?

LIZ: That's my job.

STUART: Being mother?

LIZ: Comes naturally. (*Beat.*)

STUART: Is he a good boss?

LIZ: Well, he expects a lot, but then he pays above the average. And he's very considerate sometimes. Let me go for a fortnight when my dad died. Even sent some flowers to the funeral.

STUART: That's nice.

LIZ: Yes, it was. Can I get you anything?

STUART: A Perrier. I'll get it. (*He goes to the kitchen.*) Does Cash have many women friends?

LIZ: I wouldn't know.

STUART: Oh, come on. You keep his diary. (*Beat.*) Between you and me, we used to think he might be gay. Not because of anything . . . specific. I suppose he was just a bit of a loner.

LIZ: He still is, then.

STUART: Fancy him yourself, do you?

LIZ: No! (*Beat.*)

STUART: I guess all his drive goes into this.

LIZ: Yeah. I guess so.

STUART: What a waste.

LIZ: I think he's very proud of the company.

STUART: He'd have to be.

DOOLEY *comes in, a bit drunk.*

LIZ: And where the hell d'you think you've been?

DOOLEY: Fret not, hen. I've been engaged on important business. Company business.

LIZ: In the pub.

DOOLEY: Christ, that's where deals get made.

LIZ: You're lucky Mr Cash is not back yet. Otherwise you'd be making a deal down at the broo.

DOOLEY: Och, well, if he's no back yet . . .

He goes to the kitchen and gets a beer from the fridge.

LIZ: You put that back Dooley.

DOOLEY: Go fuck yourself.

STUART: Dooley . . .(*Beat.*)

DOOLEY: Yes? (*Beat.*)

STUART: Don't talk to Liz like that. She's only doing her job.

DOOLEY: Her job is to type out wee letters and post them. Her job is to make the tea and wipe the boss's bum for him when he has a shite.

STUART: And don't get smart with me, lad.

DOOLEY *snorts.*

DOOLEY: What are you going to do about it? Going to teach me a lesson are you? Old man?

STUART: No.

DOOLEY: That's right. No. (*Beat.*)

STUART: Look, lad, you'll be out on your arse if Cash comes back.

DOOLEY: I won't be out on nothing.

STUART: Don't screw up. (*Beat.*)

LIZ: Come on, Dooley. (ROBIN *comes in.*)

DOOLEY: Oh fuck. It's the Bisto Kid.

He laughs and goes out with LIZ.

ROBIN: You've met the office yob?

STUART: Yeah.

ROBIN: Everyone has to have one. Keeps the unemployment figures healthy.

STUART: What, is he on a scheme?

ROBIN: No. Cash has taken him under his wing, so to speak.

STUART: Oh aye?

ROBIN: Oh aye. (*Beat.*) So, how's it going with you, then?

STUART: Pretty good. You?

ROBIN: Could be better. (*Beat.*) Look, I'm sorry we got off on the wrong foot.

STUART: Forget it. I have.

ROBIN: Yeah.

STUART: Are you not in on this Tory promo thing, then?

ROBIN: Not yet. I'll probably get the call if they need a few snappy one-liners. Nice and superficial. I'm busting my balls on this American Cable thing at the moment.

STUART: Sounds impressive.

ROBIN: Yeah. Twenty-four hour soft-porn TV. How d'you make that sound attractive to the government commission?

STUART: Does it show a profit?

ROBIN: Say what? Megabucks.

STUART: QED. (*Beat.*)

ROBIN: Uh . . . would you do me a favour?

STUART: If I can.

ROBIN: Well, see, I've written this . . . film script. It's not finished or anything, not properly. I wondered if you'd have a look at it for me. Tell me if I'm doing it right.

STUART: What's it about?

ROBIN: Uh . . . basically, it's about two guys who open an off-licence, then a cocktail bar, then a club. One guy's black, one's white. It's sort of a love story. (*Beat.*)

STUART: Yeah. I'll read it.

ROBIN: Great. I'll go and get a copy . . . if that's OK.

STUART: Sure.

ROBIN *goes out.* STUART *looks amused and takes the video out of the machine.* LIZ *comes in.*

LIZ: I'm sorry, Mr Clarke. Dooley's quite new.

STUART: You can say that again.

LIZ: Gives us Scots a bad name, him and his kind.

STUART: I've known enough Scots to be able to tell the difference.

ROBIN *comes in with the script and gives it to* STUART.

ROBIN: Here. No hurry. Just . . . I dunno. Let me know what you think.

STUART: This is the first script anybody's given me to read for over four years. I'll be very careful with it.

CASH *comes in looking harassed.*

CASH: Hi everyone. Stuart, I'm sorry, we said two-thirty, didn't we?

STUART: Not to worry.

CASH: Liz, coffee, please. I'm drowning in bloody brandy. Why is it that some people only seem to think you're serious if you can down half a vat of brandy after lunch? Rob? Do something for you?

ROBIN: No.

CASH: OK, then. Off you go.

ROBIN: Maybe if I wore a kilt, I might get a please.

CASH: I don't have time, Robin. Just get out and come when I buzz you. Understood?

ROBIN: Crystal. (*He goes.*)

CASH: Jesus. Why is everybody a prima donna today? Liz, where's Dooley?

LIZ: I sent him out.

CASH: Shit, why didn't you wait till I got back? (*She brings his coffee.*) I want to send him over to Tate's for some artwork.

LIZ: He won't be long. I'll tell him as soon as he gets back.

CASH: He should be here now. Wait until I'm back next time.

LIZ: I will. (*She goes.*)

CASH: What a sodding day.

STUART: Actually Cash, the reason she sent him out, was that he'd obviously had one too many for lunch and was being an obnoxious little git.

CASH: Why didn't she tell me that?

STUART: Because she's a pro. (*Beat.*)

CASH: Oh, fuck . . . (*He presses the intercom.*) Liz. Sorry.

He releases it without waiting for a reply.

OK, Stuart.

STUART: Shall I tell you what I've got?

CASH: First the bad news. I've just had lunch with . . . an old friend in the know *vis-à-vis* the toings and froings of the Conservative and Unionist Party hierarchy. Howard has been a little naughty with us. This cosy little deal we're part of is news to everyone at Smith Square. I come out looking very bad. Not to mention more than a little silly.

STUART: That's how they are. You stab my back, I'll stab yours.

CASH: Yeah, who needs it? We, apparently, are part of a concerted campaign by Howard and friends to discredit the leadership.

STUART: Oh dear . . .

CASH: Right. Some very damaging leaks have appeared in the last twelve months, yeah? Well, guess who.

STUART: Up shit creek is where we are.

CASH: Not quite. We carry on. Same brief. Different client. (*Beat.*) I sold them the package.

STUART: Nice one. And Howard?

CASH: Backbench obscurity with any luck. (*Beat.*) This is my life we're talking about. So I'm not mucking about.

STUART: Well. We're in with the big boys now.

CASH: Too right. (*He indicates* STUART*'s glass.*) Perrier?

STUART: You need a clear head when you're working for Fascists. (*They smile.*)

CASH: I'm glad you're with me. And Bright. He'll be setting the record straight this Sunday, in Fleet Street code.

STUART: Even rats have their uses.

CASH: Not nice.

STUART: I know he's not.

CASH: You could get to like him.

STUART: I could get to like ulcerative colitis. But I won't. (*Beat.*)

CASH: OK. What have you got? Talk to me, baby.

DOOLEY *comes in.*

Dooley, run that over to Tate's.

He gives him an envelope.

DOOLEY: What, the noo?

CASH: Yes, 'the noo' (DOOLEY *sways.*) And then go home. Take the afternoon off. (DOOLEY *stands there.*) What?

DOOLEY: I'll need a key.

STUART *pretends not to hear.* CASH *gives a key to* DOOLEY *who goes.*

STUART: Right, the idea I have here, very much planning stage at the moment, is that we concentrate on the opposition. Because I'll be perfectly frank, Cash, I hate the bloody sight of Thatcher and Tebbit. And I reckon so does a goodly portion of the nation at large. Their material's thin. They need to be used sparingly.

CASH: Yes, but they do need to be used.

STUART: I thought you said 'same brief'.

CASH: Same brief, different . . . emphasis. Can you handle it?

STUART: Oh yes. I can handle it.

CASH: Good. (*Beat.*)

STUART: Anyway I've had a whale of a time, going through archive stuff, and I've come up with a potted history of the labour movement in revolt since about 1965. Now, to me, this stuff is beautiful. There's Saltley. Arthur looking great. Heath looking like a twat, not difficult to find that one. All the Vietnam stuff. Lots of coppers getting booted. Winter of discontent. Strikes, marches, punch-ups. And d'you know what's most beautiful about it? It's all in black and white. It's the fucking ark! What is black and white? Black and white is Old, it's depressing, it's the Past. Now, you intercut pictures of opposition leaders, also in black and white, with appropriate quotes, but, every time you mention this fucking awful Government's record, you switch to colour, Fists, blood, blah-blah, black and white. New technology, sunrise industry: glorious colour. Trade unions, strikes, power failures: black and white. Home ownership, the Falklands: living bloody sensurround. (*Beat.*) I hate it. But I love it.

CASH: Sounds good. Sounds very good.

STUART: I know. Look, in the good old days, people got their information from newspapers, or by word of mouth, or pamphlets or whatever. There was probably much less information flying around, but people used their own faculties, their own experiences to form their attitudes to things, right? Well, the arrival of the news camera, the broadcast, changed all that. Suddenly, the public were there. Part of the action. Observers. Except, when you're really there, you can move about, get a general picture. But, the picture the public gets is the one the cameraman's getting. So, it's simple. Think of a picket line. You ever been on a picket, Cash?

CASH: Stuart, please.

STUART: OK, so imagine it. Get the image. What'd you see? (*Beat.*)

CASH: Strikers, banners . . .

STUART: Yeah . . .

CASH: Police . . .

STUART: Where?

CASH: Hmmm?

STUART: Where are the police?

CASH: Oh. In front of me.

STUART: Between you and the pickets.

CASH: Yeah.

STUART: Protecting you, right?

CASH: If you like.

STUART: It's a simple point. Can you ever remember the camera making you feel a part of the picket line? That those people around you were protecting you, your job?

CASH: No. But then, that wouldn't be objective, impartial reporting, would it? (*He smiles.*)

STUART: I'm a film-maker. I know the camera's never neutral. So. Over the years, what we've seen is the gradual assimilation of the general public into the ranks of the defenders of property. The public's so-called objective position is with the police, the bosses, the government, capital. The camera has given the silent majority its politics. The politics of the State. (*Beat.*) That is what I want to exploit in this broadcast. It'll be very good. You can trust me, I'm a doctor.

CASH: So the whole thing'll have a newsy, documentary feel to it.

STUART: Totally. Make it like a news broadcast. Use news pictures. Tap that deep-rooted response. Labour is violence, chaos, fear.

CASH: We're not talking subtlety here, I take it.

STUART: No. (*Beat.*) The only alternative I could come up with was ten minutes of Geoffrey Howe defending the Government's record. Instant valium.

CASH: So. It is true.

STUART: What?

CASH: There really is no alternative.

STUART: There is also no business like show business. (*Beat.*)

CASH: What about sound? Voice over?

STUART: Authoritative. Doom-laden. Get the bloke who does the nuclear warning. And music. Grand and heavy. Scare the public shitless. (*Beat.*) You said think Goebbels.

CASH: I didn't know you had it in you. You're not just selling out. You're having a grand closing-down sale.

STUART: Yeah. Everything must go. (*He's down for a moment.*) What d'you reckon?

CASH: I like it. A lot. I think you've cracked it. Well done. We'll run it by Eric, then I think we might run with it.

STUART: I've still got loads of archive stuff to go through. Between you and me, I'm trying to turn up a shot of Bright at a miners' gala.

CASH: You'll be lucky. When d'you think you can have a mock-up for me?

STUART: Couple of days, tops.

CASH: That's great. (*He pours a coffee.*) Coffee?

STUART: No thanks.

CASH: How are things at home? How's Amanda?

STUART: OK. (*Beat.*) Listen, I need . . . some advice . . . help, I suppose.

CASH: I'm not being funny mate, but . . . not in office hours, eh?

STUART (*beat*): I reckon . . . I'm pretty

certain . . . she's been having an affair. (*Beat.*) I know she's not happy. With her job, with me. She hasn't been for a while. (*Beat.*) Every now and again I try to make contact again. Go on the wagon. Be nice. Be whoever it is she wants me to be. It never lasts. She won't meet me half way. I get the feeling sometimes that she doesn't actually like me. Me. Who I am deep down. I mean, I don't always like myself. I let me down a lot. But I always find I have a sneaking residual regard for myself. (*Beat.*) I'm not a bad man.

CASH: Maybe just not good enough.

STUART: Yeah. I want to make it work. I don't know how.

CASH: You're asking the wrong man. I'm not exactly a paragon of family virtue. (*Beat.*)

STUART: What's it like, being on your own?

CASH: It has its moments. Its compensations.

STUART: I don't think I could face it. (*Beat.*) That's why I'm doing this, y'know. For Amanda. That's why I want it to be good.

CASH: It's a good enough reason.

STUART: It's the best.

GILL *comes into reception.*

CASH: I hope it works out.

STUART: So do I, mate. Because if it doesn't . . .

GILL *enters.*

CASH: Gillian, hello.

GILL: Hello.

CASH: Just keep at it then, Stuart.

STUART: Yeah. (*Beat. He smiles.*) Right-wing thinking. It ought to have a government health warning. (*He goes.*)

CASH: Hard to believe, but he's the nearest thing to a genius I've ever met.

GILL: He doesn't seem very happy.

CASH: They never are. That's left to us ordinary mortals. Can I get you anything? Drink?

GILL: No, I like to . . . keep a clear

head. Nothing, thanks.

CASH: OK. (*He offers her a seat.*) I'm sorry we never got a chance to go through your interview.

GILL: So am I.

CASH: Howard's of the old school. I'm sorry.

GILL: That's all right. He'll pay. (*Beat.*)

CASH: Yes. (*Beat.*)

GILL: One hears whispers.

CASH: Oh?

GILL: All very malicious, probably. (*Beat.*)

CASH: Right. The interview. I just want to give you some presentation points. Nothing to do with the substance, that's not my area.

GILL: Don't you have any political beliefs, Mr Cash? (*Beat.*)

CASH: Oh yes.

GILL: What are they?

CASH: Not far removed from yours. More . . .

GILL: What?

CASH: I was going to say: more ruthless, perhaps.

GILL: Oh, don't let my sex fool you. I'm as ruthless as any man.

CASH: You'll go far. (*He smiles.*)

GILL: Let's hope so. (*She smiles.*) Have you ever thought of standing for office?

CASH: Often.

GILL: Then why not? Not lack of ambition, surely.

CASH: Far from it. My problem is I don't think I could keep up the public face. I think I might look like I was enjoying myself too much. I might look a little . . . smug. Cruel, even. Something a politician can't afford.

GILL: I understand.

CASH: That's something you have to look out for.

GILL: It's difficult, though, when you know you're right, don't you find?

CASH: I do. But I'm not after peoples'

votes. And that's the name of the game. Making yourself attractive and credible to the voters.

GILL: Mr Cash, you're a cynic.

CASH: Probably. But I'm right.

GILL: I must think about it.

LIZ *appears at the door.*

LIZ: Sorry. I've got Mr Benson on the line.

CASH: Damn. Uh, look . . . get his number, tell him I'll get straight back to him.

LIZ: OK. (*She goes.*)

CASH: Damn.

GILL: I'm sorry, if I'm . . .

CASH: No, it's just somebody I've been trying to track down.

GILL: Look . . . why don't we meet up again? Somewhere more relaxed. (*Beat.*)

CASH: Lunch? Dinner?

GILL: Dinner would be nice. (*Beat.*) Why don't you call me at the hotel?

CASH: Yes. I will. (*Beat.*)

GILL: I think we'll find lots to talk about. There's a lot I want to learn.

CASH: I'll do my best. (*He stands.*)

GILL: I'm a very determined woman, Mr Cash.

CASH: I admire that.

GILL: Good. I'll be off, then.

CASH: Right.

GILL: Goodbye.

She goes. LIZ comes in. She gives him a piece of paper.

CASH: Get Robin for me, will you, Liz?

She stands and gives him a look.

What?

LIZ: I don't like her.

CASH (*smiles*): I know. isn't she absolutely bloody awful?!

He laughs. LIZ goes.

Blackout.

Scene Three

Evening, a week later. The kitchen table is spread with buffet food. There are bottles of wine and champagne. In the lobby are CASH, LIZ, ROBIN, GILL, ERIC *and* AMANDA, *drinks in hand, looking at the pictures on the wall and talking.* STUART, *in the office, pops a bottle of champagne. He's a bit drunk.* AMANDA *comes in. She too is slightly drunk.*

AMANDA (*seeing STUART*): Oh God. (*Beat.*)

STUART: What? (*Beat.*) I don't know why he doesn't just write a cheque for ten grand, frame it and stick it up on the wall. There's no need to bother with all that paint and canvas. Messy bloody stuff. A good crisp Barclay's cheque. That's all he needs. (*She pours a drink.*) After all, he has the artistic appreciation of a brain-damaged two-toed sloth.

AMANDA: How do you know?

STUART: We go back a long way. We're old muckers.

AMANDA: You didn't know Cash fifteen years ago and you don't now. You never bothered.

STUART: D'you blame me? (*Beat.*) Have you ever looked into his eyes? Which are the windows of the soul? Have you? I have. I peered in and saw all these pricey pictures and nobody home.

AMANDA: I thought you weren't going to drink?

STUART: Celebration, isn't it? Anyway, you're pushing it back.

AMANDA: I'm allowed. I'm not an alcoholic. (*Beat.*)

STUART: D'you know what he was telling me about the other day? Banking. Advertising jargon and banking. D'you know what a high net-worth individual is? I didn't. Well. A high net-worth individual is a rich bastard. Yeah. And, d'you know what they call banking for people who aren't high net-worth individuals? People who are, in fact, poor? D'you know? It's called cloth-cap banking. (*Beat.*) Don't you just love it? (*Beat.*)

AMANDA: Stuart. Behave. Please.

STUART: Why?

AMANDA: I don't know. When in Rome?

STUART: Bollocks. When in Rome, act like a cunt. (Eric *comes in,*.) Talking of which . . .

ERIC: Letting it all hang out, Clarkie?

STUART: In short, yes. Brightie.

ERIC (*dialling the phone, to* AMANDA): I love this man. A joy to work with. Never a dull moment.

STUART: That's what you think. I had a few, I can tell you. The dullest has got to be Brightie giving me the gen on popular capitalism. How it's the saviour of Great Britain and all who sail in her. That was dull. Very, very dull.

AMANDA: You, of course, are never less than rivetting.

ERIC *is speaking into the phone.*

STUART: Hey, less of the smut if you don't mind. (*Beat.*) Who you calling, Brightie? Eh? Heavy breathing to the blessed Margaret? A bit of insider trading?

ERIC *puts the phone down.*

ERIC: Minicab, actually.

STUART: Minicab? I had you down as a Roller man. Merc at the very least.

ERIC: Can't leave the Rolls in the car park at Heathrow, can I? It would only get vandalised by a disaffected member of the progressive class.

STUART: With any luck.

AMANDA: Where are you flying?

ERIC: Montserrat. Fact finding freebie for the Colour Supp.

STUART: He likes to keep his ear close to the ground. Find out what the chap in Club Class is thinking.

AMANDA: It's supposed to be beautiful there.

ERIC: I hope so.

STUART: I don't. I can't imagine you with a real tan.

AMANDA: We've never been anywhere like that, have we?

STUART (*thinking hard*): I don't know. Is it anything like Barnsley?

ERIC: Not especially.

STUART: Well then, I don't think we've been anywhere like that.

AMANDA: No.

STUART: I took you to Derry. Ungrateful bag.

AMANDA (*looks upset*): Yes. I forgot. Thanks.

He raises his hand in a gesture of apology but says nothing. LIZ *comes in.*

LIZ: Everyone OK?

AMANDA: Fine, thanks.

ERIC: I'd love a Guinness.

STUART: Me too. Sabrina. That's the one I'd like.

AMANDA: Oh God . . .

LIZ: I thought you were reformed, Mr Clarke.

STUART: This isn't really happening. It's a nightmare. Nothing is real.

LIZ: That's all right then. (*She gives* ERIC *his drink and goes.*)

ERIC: Nectar of the gods. Dublin –

STUART: – brewed. Nothing like it. (*Beat.*) You got shares in Guinness or something?

ERIC: Yes. (*Beat. They both laugh.*) See. We *can* get on.

STUART: I haven't got the energy to hate you, Brightie.

ERIC: That's good.

STUART: Is it?

AMANDA: You're all the same. Get a couple of drinks inside you and it's all chaps together. The saloon bar brotherhood. Bloody men.

STUART: My wife's hatred, on the other hand, knows no bounds. She can hate. My God, how she can hate. Bring down a man at a hundred paces with her hatred, she can.

AMANDA: Most men seem perfectly capable of bringing themselves down, thank you very much.

STUART (*bitter*): But you just love to give us a little nudge.

ERIC: Do I detect a whiff of cordite in the air?

STUART: No. Just the embers of a fire that went out.

Again, AMANDA *is visibly upset. She goes out and joins the others in the lobby.*

ERIC: Tell me, Clarkie, pre-brewer's droop, were you a whips and chains man?

STUART: Do what?

ERIC: The black leather hood. Manacles in the cellar. Fag butts on the chest.

STUART: You feeling all right?

ERIC: Mas-o-chism. (*Beat.*) You do seem to enjoy a good frolic in the broken glass.

STUART: Oh. I dunno. (*Beat.*) Fuck it.

He goes and opens another bottle of champagne. ROBIN *comes in.*

ROBIN: Art fatigue already?

STUART: What Cash knows about art could be written on the back of a cheque stub. In fact, probably is.

ROBIN: But he knows what he likes.

STUART: I wonder.

ERIC: Why is it that people like Cash and myself attract such venom from the left-wing, artist class? Is it because we achieve? Grammar boys in a comprehensive world? Because we make money? Fine for the printer, not for the journalist? Because we don't swallow the old orthodoxies? What? What is this heinous crime we've committed?

STUART: You're a couple of mercenary shitbags.

ERIC: God, is that all?!

STUART: Yes. That's all.

ROBIN: Whoah, time out. Left-wing, artist class, moi? *Nyet*, comrades. What you see before you is the new man. No-wing, hedonist, post-industrial, post-modern –

STUART: Post early for Christmas.

ROBIN (*mocking*): Style. Dancing on the ruins. It's a hit and run culture. Bizarre connections. Stop making sense. Death to syntax. Long live the slogan. I'm talkin' bout my generation, daddio.

STUART *guffaws and comes down to* ROBIN.

STUART (*putting his arm round* ROBIN's *shoulder*): Oh, I love this boy. He means it, he really means it. He reckons his jacket is a political statement. And d'you know what, Brightie? He's not afraid to put his money where his designer boxer shorts are. This boy has given me a film script. This cultural buzz-saw has written a piece for the modern cinema. Post-modern cinema, sorry. And d'you know what? It's a love story. A love story! About two blokes, agreed, but that's not exactly risqué in these days of Sodom and Gomorrah, is it? I was expecting Fellini, Bukowski, Burroughs, Buñuel at the very least. And what did I get? A polyunsaturated Colin Welland. An absolute beginner! (*Beat.*) And we're going to make the film, aren't we?

ROBIN (*smiling*): That's right.

STUART: I love him!

He plants a smacker on ROBIN's *forehead as* AMANDA *comes in.*

AMANDA: Now that is grounds for divorce.

STUART: You don't want to divorce me. It's too much fun watching me twitch around with my wings pulled off.

AMANDA: Fun? Now there's a novel concept. (*Beat.*) C'mon, Paul wants your opinion on something.

STUART: *Paul* wants *my* opinion?

AMANDA: All right then, *I* want your opinion. Your company. Your presence.

STUART: My balls.

AMANDA: I've got 'em.

STUART: Yeah.

AMANDA: C'mon.

He goes off with her, taking a champagne bottle.

ERIC: You say you're making the film. Is that for real?

ROBIN: Yuh.

ERIC: You've got finance?

ROBIN: Yuh. TV tie-in.

ERIC: Well, good luck with it. (*Beat.*) And it's about two blokes, is it?

ROBIN: Yuh.

ERIC: Interesting. (*Beat.*) You don't get a lot of films like that.

ROBIN: Oh, I don't know.

ERIC: Well I don't see many like that.

ROBIN: Obviously you don't go to the right places.

ERIC: Obviously. (*Beat.*) It's a shame you weren't in on the broadcast with us. It would have been nice to work together.

ROBIN: Politics isn't exactly my strong suit. I'm easily bored.

ERIC: Oh, absolutely. That's why I gave up Parliament. I mean, everybody seems to think I did it for money, but it's not true. Not entirely. I did it because it was so boring. The shiny trouser seats. The dandruff on the collars. The shabby, boring ritual of democracy: a lot of middle-aged men reeking of mothballs and stale whisky; a total sham. There comes a point where you're sitting there, and you look around, and you think: am I really a misfit like the rest of them? You look at your colleagues and you find them excruciatingly embarrassing, and you realise that other sane people must be looking at *you* like that. And you think: show me to the exit. So I made my excuses and left. (*Beat.*) All the interesting folk have gone. There's only the bores and the lonely left. (*Beat.*) I find the real world so much more stimulating.

ROBIN: Yuh. Me too. (*Beat.*)

ERIC: Listen, Robin. When I get back from Montserrat, what do you say we meet up. Dinner maybe. I know some very interesting people from your point of view.

ROBIN: Uh . . .

ERIC: TV, films. All very necessary if you want to go big time.

ROBIN: Sure. Look, Mr Bright . . .

ERIC: Eric . . .

ROBIN: Eric . . . about the film. The two blokes thing.

ERIC (*laughing*): Robin, Robin, don't say what I think you're going to say.

ROBIN: I just don't want any misunderstanding.

ERIC: What's to misunderstand?

ROBIN: Well, if you write about a gay theme, people sort of assume . . .

ERIC: I never assume. Assumptions are the death of spontaneity. (*Beat.*) So. Don't worry. I'm not assuming you're gay.

ROBIN: Oh no, it's not that. It's just . . .

ERIC: What?

ROBIN: Well . . . I don't fancy you. (*Beat.*)

There is noise from the lobby. DOOLEY lurches into the room, followed by CASH and LIZ. He goes straight for the champagne.

DOOLEY: You cannae have a party without Dooley. I am vital to the smooth running of any social function. Am I no right, boss?

He swigs from the bottle. CASH smiles, trying to placate him.

CASH: Yes. But you have to keep it nice.

DOOLEY: Nice? Fucking nice? Get to fuck . . .

CASH: Because if you don't, you get your bottom smacked.

DOOLEY: Ooh, I am all aquiver.

ERIC (*amiable*): Trouble with the staff?

CASH: Over-exuberance.

DOOLEY: Bollocks to that. I'm on drugs, you bampot.

LIZ: Dooley . . .

DOOLEY: What is it, hen? You want a

good shagging?

CASH: OK, that's it.

DOOLEY: Don't you come anywhere fucking near me. I am not your property.

CASH: You're fired.

DOOLEY: You did that already.

CASH: I'm just reminding you.

STUART, AMANDA *and* GILL *come in.*

STUART: Cash, who sold you that bullshit?

CASH: It was a commission.

STUART: You actually paid someone to paint it? Jesus. I didn't know you were involved in charity for the blind.

CASH: It's an investment.

STUART: Then put it in the bloody bank. Get it out of sight.

GILL: I think it's rather good.

STUART: Are we speaking artistically or financially here?

GILL: I would say it conforms to certain traditional rules, and as such, is pleasing to the eye.

There is a general frisson at this. STUART *giggles.*

Yes, I know you'll mock, but that's what I feel.

STUART: And you obviously feel things very deeply.

GILL: Some things, yes.

ERIC: Surely it's all in the eye of the beholder.

STUART: Christ, Brightie, with a penetrating and original mind like yours, how come when you ratted on Labour, you never joined the SDP?

ERIC: I'm not principled enough.

STUART: You said it.

LIZ *is bringing round a tray of food.*

God, Liz, don't wait on me. I hate it.

LIZ: It's what I do. It's what I'm paid for.

STUART: Well don't do it at me.

CASH: Don't you find your social conscience a bit of a millstone, Stuart?

STUART: It's nothing to do with conscience. It's demeaning.

GILL: But everybody has to work. Somebody has to do the waiting.

STUART: *You* do it, then. Or let's see Nigel Lawson's daughter cleaning toilets. Mark Thatcher washing cars for a quid an hour.

ERIC: Oh, Clarkie, you're so tribal. So socialist.

AMANDA: Huh.

STUART: What's wrong with that? It's not illegal. Yet.

ERIC: Everything's wrong with it. It's what's wrong with the whole bloody country.

GILL: Hear hear.

ERIC: I mean, you're an intelligent man, Stuart. A talented man. Yet you waste your talent desperately trying to dupe the people into swallowing your idiotic vision of a New Jerusalem. I've seen your vision. It's grotesque. It's sentimental. It's a bloody lie. (*Beat.*) Christ, how can a country ever progress if a whole group of people like yourself explode with apoplexy at the injustice of the class system every time they're offered a canapé? It's not rational.

STUART: Neither is exploitation.

ERIC *laughs.*

ERIC: Leaving aside the fact that I disagree, look at Liz, Stuart. Does she look exploited?

LIZ *gives him a fierce look.*

No. She doesn't. She's simply doing a job of work.

AMANDA: She's not a specimen, Eric.

LIZ: I can speak for myself.

AMANDA: Well, excuse me.

ERIC: She sells her labour. We all do. It's nothing to be ashamed of. She's hardworking and loyal. Those are virtues. Not things to be sneered at.

STUART: I'm sure you've never noticed, but that's what socialism's all about.

ERIC: Oh God. Not socialism. *Again.* If
only we could wave a wand, make it
disappear. Chant a spell, or something.
Socialism's irrelevant.

CASH: It's also destructive.

ERIC: Absolutely. It *is* an alien ideology.
The majority of people neither
understand nor want it. It hangs over
us all like a black cloud, desperately
kept aloft by the huffing and puffing of
the activists. Oh, the activists. The
great fat cuckoos in the Labour nest. A
nice left-of-centre party, with sensible
managerial policies, totally hijacked by
a combination of the sentimentally
gullible, yourself, and the beady-eyed
fanatics, the revolutionaries. Let's face
it, socialism's not on the agenda, old
fruit. It's history. The people are
scared to death of it.

AMANDA: You, of course, would know
all about the people and what they
want. With your intimate knowledge of
them. From your Channel Island tax
haven and your pied-à-terre in
Bloomsbury. I think, if you were to be
completely honest, you'd have to say
that you're making educated guesses
based on self-interest and innate
prejudice. Oh, I know those are the
perfect qualifications for membership
of your little club, the Sunday
pontificator's, but they're sod all to do
with the real world. God, we used to
go to church to be preached at and told
what was wrong and what was right.
Now we just open the paper and up
pops the pulpit and there's little Eric
Bright telling it how it really is. You
and your little chums, all barking away
together. D'you know what you make
me think of when you're on your soap
box? D'you know what I see? I see
good lunches. Fine wine. And great fat
cigars (*Beat.*) You're the self-appointed
loudhailers for a government that's
turned this country into a land fit for
Rupert Murdoch.

GILL: What an utterly absurd statement.

AMANDA: Oh . . . naff off. It amazes
me that you'll all give credence to this
dim-witted country cow, who, after the
next election will almost certainly be a
Member of Parliament for Christ's
sake, and yet you pour all the shit you

can on the idea, just the idea, of
socialism. Well, it's not the people who
are scared of socialism, it's you.
Because it would drop your lovely
lunch in your lap, and stick your great
fat cigar up your arse.

GILL: Is this what passes for politics
where you come from? Foulmouthed
abuse?

AMANDA: You want politics, sister? I'll
give you politics. Not my husband's
soggy labourist crap. That's just Tory
paternalism with a collectivist face.
Thanks to their silly soft-centre
deference we still live in one of the
most class-ridden, tradition-bound
societies in the modern world. A living
museum of obsolescence. You can't
tamper with it. You can't reform it.
You have to replace it.

ERIC: Don't tell me your wife's a Trot,
Clarkie.

STUART: I don't know.

AMANDA: No, you bloody don't.
(*Beat.*) Socialism hasn't failed Britain.
It's never been tried. It's axiomatic that
the Labour Party has only ever wrung
concessions from capital, not
challenged it.

ERIC: Someone's been reading her *New
Left Review.*

AMANDA: I used to write for it, you
condescending shithead.

CASH: Amanda . . .

AMANDA: I'm sick of it. Your little
parliamentary game. Your boys' club
with it's crappy rules and its honorary
men. Pretending to be alternatives to
each other. Well, you're all petrified.
Every last one of you. Petrified of
anything that'd shake you out of your
cosy embrace. You want politics,
sister? Let's spend the seven thousand
pounds it costs to keep someone
unemployed on training, on generating
employment, on investment. Let's
spend the six thousand million pounds
we'll get from North Sea oil every year
for the next decade on converting
dangerous and wasteful industry, on
rehabilitating the health service. Let's
have human control of economic
forces. Decent priorities. Devolve.

Decentralise. Because if we don't, if we just sit on our hands and wait for the world economy to show signs of growth, then we're all going down the tubes. Condemned as a complacent, cowardly, decayed parody of an industrial country. Oh, and freedom? Dissent? Imagination? Luxuries. Irrelevant to their plans. It's a prison state. The Establishment are the warders. You lot are the trusties, darlings. (*Beat.*) Alien, or what?

DOOLEY *swings round with the video camera in his hand.*

DOOLEY: I cannae understand a word you people say. You make a lot of noise, but I don't get any meaning from it.

ROBIN: For once, we agree.

CASH: It's called conversation.

ERIC: Cut and thrust.

DOOLEY: Oh aye? Well the only cut and thrust I know is with a broken bottle.

GILL: Really . . .

DOOLEY *goes over to her.*

DOOLEY: Really . . . Who are you? *What* are you?

He points the camera at her. Her face comes up on the screen.

Are you a very important person? A VIP?

Beat. He points it at AMANDA.

And you? What are you?

AMANDA: Oh go away.

DOOLEY: Ooh, I like you.

Beat. He points the camera at CASH *and then at* ROBIN.

Well. I think we know all about you two.

Beat. He points it at ERIC.

You. I've seen *you* on the box. Yap yap yap. I've seen you. But . . . I don't know what you *do*. I mean, Leslie Crowther, I know what he does. He gives people suites of furniture and mopeds. Les Dawson, he gives them a Blankety Blank cheque book. But *you*. What do you give away?

ERIC: Nothing.

DOOLEY: Then what the fuck are you doing on my television set?! (*Beat.*) When I lived at home with my family, I used to watch the TV all day. And I can tell you what good television is. It's where they give you something. You wave your arms about and act like a prat and you win a prize. Fucking great, eh? Well, where's my prize? I've come all the way to London to win something and all I've got is a cardboard box to sleep in and a lot of men playing with my willy. Somebody tell Bob Monkhouse. Tell him what it's really like. (*He turns the camera on himself.*) Look, I'm on TV. Look, there I am. Ask me a question. Ask me where I'm from. What do I do for a living? Actually I'm unemployed at the moment. Aaaah. No, I'm not married, Cilla, but I wouldn't mind poking you, eh? I like windsurfing and I fuck dogs. Now, gimme a prize. I'm on. I want something. *You owe me* something! (*Beat.*) I'm on . . . you bastards.

CASH *takes the camera from him and hands it to* ROBIN.

You've got everything, you, and you won't give me a prize.

CASH *turns round suddenly, giving* DOOLEY *a backhanded belt across the face.* DOOLEY *goes flying. The others gasp etc.* CASH *picks* DOOLEY *up, blood round his mouth.*

Mind the fucking suit . . .

CASH: It's mine. I paid.

He throws DOOLEY *onto the sofa. People are shocked. Nobody does anything.*

LIZ: Mr Cash . . .

CASH: Job training, Liz.

He picks DOOLEY *up and thumps him in the stomach.*

STUART: Stop it, Cash . . .

DOOLEY (*hardly able to speak*): It's not even my own clothes I'm bleeding on.

He laughs. CASH *hits him in the face again.*

AMANDA: Make him stop.

CASH *lifts him up.*

CASH: I owe you nothing! Nobody owes anybody else a thing. Got me?

DOOLEY (*laughing*): Lend us a fiver . . .

CASH *is about to hit him again. LIZ suddenly steps in and grabs DOOLEY away. ROBIN rushes out. STUART helps LIZ lift DOOLEY. CASH goes to the kitchen and pops a bottle of champagne. ERIC has looked at his watch and out the window.*

ERIC: Is it written on tablets of stone somewhere that minicabs will always be late?

Beat. GILL goes to CASH and fills her glass.

STUART: You really believe it, don't you, Cash? Nobody owes anybody else a thing!

CASH: Having studied all the available evidence, yes.

STUART: You've studied nothing. You're working from instinct. Lust. That's why you're such a vicious bastard.

CASH: I operate, Stuart, that's all. Nothing new, nothing special in that. But it means I don't have time for the emotional garbage people like you carry round. I won't be trapped like you. I won't let you trap me. I'll just operate. And screw the cost.

STUART: It'll come back to you. It always does.

CASH: Not if you keep moving.

STUART: It'll get you. Even if it's just one night where you wake up, and the dark frightens you.

CASH: I'll sleep with the light on.

STUART: Very smart.

CASH: I like to think so. (*Beat.*)

STUART: You'll never understand, will you? You haven't got the humanity to understand.

GILL (*pointing at DOOLEY*): Are we supposed to understand that?

STUART: Yes!

AMANDA: Patronising bastard.

STUART: Not now. Please. (*Beat.*)

LIZ *stands DOOLEY up. He's in a bad way.*

LIZ: Come on . . .

STUART: Need a hand?

AMANDA: Don't you run out now.

STUART: He's in pain, for Christ's sake.

AMANDA: Well, you're not going to stop that. You'll only be making yourself feel good.

LIZ: Fuck you . . .

She walks DOOLEY out.

STUART: Doesn't hide it, does it? All the high-tech. It's still a fucking jungle.

CASH: What did you expect?

STUART: Oh, God, I dunno. What did I expect? Nothing, I suppose. (*Beat.*) What did I want? (*Beat.*) Love. (*Beat.*) This . . . ruthlessness. It's not human, that's all.

CASH: You see, that's your mistake. It is human. Quintessentially bloody human. You're a freak of nature. You've forgotten you're an animal.

STUART: Yeah. It's what's known as civilisation.

AMANDA *sits by him. HOWARD suddenly appears, very upset.*

HOWARD: Ah. (*Beat.*)

CASH: Howard.

ERIC *looks out the window.*

ERIC: At last. (*He gets his bag.*) Can't stop, Howard, my cab's here. I'll call you next week, Paul.

CASH: OK.

ERIC's *almost gone.*

HOWARD: You're a treacherous bastard, Bright.

ERIC *stops, half-turns and looks as if he's going to reply, then he smiles.*

ERIC: Yes, see you then. (*He goes.*)

HOWARD: And as for you two . . .

CASH: What can I do for you, Howard?

HOWARD: Take the knife out from between my shoulder-blades.

CASH: Oh, come on . . .

HOWARD *takes out a photo wallet.*

HOWARD: Look. My wife. My children. Do you know what you've done to them?

CASH: Frankly, no.

HOWARD: Joint effort, was it? The two of you cook it up together?

CASH: Who?

HOWARD: You and the wicked witch here.

CASH: Gill? What's she got to do with it?

HOWARD: Oh Jesus, spare me that one, please. OK, Cash, you get a better offer, fair enough, do some politicking of your own. That I can take. That, I possibly even expect. But why, dear God, why drag me all the way down?

CASH: I changed clients, that's all. You hadn't been exactly honest with me, Howard. In fact you could have ruined me.

HOWARD: So you ruined me.

CASH: I changed clients. And Eric wrote a small piece. Hardly treacherous.

HOWARD: And what about the fact that I am now officially branded a criminal? (*Beat.*)

CASH: Sorry, Howard, not with you.

HOWARD: I'll draw you a bloody map, shall I? I have just been forced to offer my resignation. Due to ill health. Didn't know I was ill? No, it came as a surprise to me as well. I was accused of an abuse of my position. I was accused of a criminal offence. To stop it going public, I had to resign. That was the price. I am no longer a Member of Parliament. I'm now an irrelevance. Finished.

CASH: But why?

HOWARD: God, because this woman accused me of raping her. (*Beat.*)

CASH: Ah.

HOWARD: Is that all you can say?

CASH: Well . . . (*Beat.*)

HOWARD: And so, they're rid of me. Opposition, y'see. They know it's a lie.

GILL: I beg your pardon, but they do not know that it's a lie. Because it isn't a lie. You're a filthy animal who takes advantage of his power to compromise women Party members in order to secure sexual favours. I risked great harm to my personal and professional reputation to expose you. However, I felt it was something I had to do, if only to protect other women like myself.

HOWARD: For Christ's sake, somebody switch her off! (*Beat.*) Listen to me you tart, you disgusting automaton, I'm going to do everything I can to ruin you. My life is shattered, all for the sake of an afternoon in the sack with a whore on the make. For that, I've lost everything. (*Beat.*) I've got a wife at home who hasn't stopped crying for two days. Three children who are going to have to live the rest of their lives with whispers and innuendoes about their father. You don't do that to somebody and expect to get away scot free. I'll drag you down. I have friends. People with influence. I'll see to it that nobody in the party will ever trust you.

GILL: You're a bad loser. That's a flaw in a politician.

HOWARD: I think I have a right to be a bad loser, considering I've lost everything.

CASH: Come on, Howard, that's not strictly true. At last count you had, what, four company directorships, a thriving family business, and homes on three continents. Hardly destitute.

HOWARD: And the disgrace?

CASH: What about it? Probably do your reputation good in some quarters. (*Beat.*) You thought you were invincible. You underestimated the stakes. Fatal. Old boy. (*Pause.*)

AMANDA: I'm sure it won't hurt for very long. Have some champers.

She holds the bottle up. HOWARD *starts to cry.*

Oh God . . .

HOWARD: My whole life . . . gone . . .

STUART: You're only out of a job.

AMANDA: Now you know how it feels.

Beat. HOWARD *looks at them and goes out.*

GILL: What a pathetic individual.

AMANDA: You should know.

CASH: Did you shop him?

GILL: Yes, of course.

CASH: Harsh.

GILL: You think so? (*Beat.*)

CASH: No.

GILL: Good. (*Beat.*) I have to go. My fiancé's picking me up at the hotel. We're driving back to Suffolk.

CASH: Give him my regards.

GILL: I will, thanks. (*To* AMANDA *and* STUART.) I hope you can come to terms with what we're doing.

STUART: Or else?

AMANDA: Up against the wall.

GILL: I don't think so. Well. Wouldn't be very English, would it? Goodbye. (*She goes.*)

AMANDA: Stuart . . . oh God . . . I want to confess something. (*Beat.*) I've had an affair. (*Beat.*) I'm sorry.

CASH *stares straight ahead.*

STUART: Had. Is it finished? (*Beat.*)

AMANDA: Oh yes.

CASH *stands and goes out.*

STUART: It hurts.

AMANDA: I know. (*Beat.*)

STUART: What do we do now?

AMANDA: Christ, I don't know.

STUART: Do we have another go?

AMANDA: I don't really know what I want any more. I just feel drained, and angry.

STUART: What can you do about it?

AMANDA: I don't know. (*Beat.*)

STUART: Between the two of us, we don't know very much at all, do we?

AMANDA: Nothing that's of any use. (*Beat.*) Let's . . . 'have another go'.

STUART: OK.

CASH *comes back in with some papers.*

CASH: Might as well get on with some work.

ROBIN *comes in and gives* CASH *an envelope.*

What is it?

ROBIN: Resignation.

CASH: Why? (ROBIN *shrugs.*) Another job?

ROBIN: Sort of.

STUART: It's my fault, Cash. He gave me a script. I showed it to David at Channel Four. We go into production in October.

CASH: You finished it.

ROBIN: It was finished all the time. (*Beat.*) I've got a couple of commissions as well.

CASH: Well done. (*Beat.*) Well. (*He extends his hand.*) Good luck.

They shake.

ROBIN: See you in the movies.

He goes. STUART *stands.*

STUART: Sorry I won't get to do the broadcast.

CASH: You've done all the work. I can get a hack in.

STUART: Well. It's been really real.

CASH: You don't have to go.

STUART (*looking round the room*): Oh . . . I think I do. (*To* AMANDA.) Fancy a meal?

AMANDA: Japanese?

STUART: You're paying.

AMANDA: OK. (*She stands.*)

CASH: Take some champagne.

STUART: No. You keep it. For a celebration.

CASH: There's still work for you, if you want it.

STUART: I'm gonna be a bit busy, as a matter of fact.

CASH: Sure.

STUART: Thanks.

CASH: Nice to see you again, Amanda.

AMANDA: Same here.

CASH: Keep the faith.

AMANDA: What else is there to do? (*Beat.*) C'mon.

They go. CASH surveys the room. LIZ comes in and starts clearing up. DOOLEY comes in holding his stomach.

CASH: Did I hurt you?

DOOLEY (*trying to smile*): Get tae fuck.

CASH: You can take it.

DOOLEY: Aye.

He takes a bottle of champagne and curls up on the sofa.

CASH: Leave it, Liz.

LIZ: It's got to be done.

She starts washing up. CASH sits at his desk.

CASH: First thing tomorrow, I want to chase Benson. (*The phone rings.*) And don't forget I'm at Smith Square in the afternoon. (*The answering machine goes on.*) So, anything urgent, you can get me there.

He switches the answering machine speaker on. LIZ's message is just finishing.

LIZ: – as soon as possible. Thank you for calling. (*The machine beeps.*)

BERKOWITZ: Cash, hi Berkowitz, New York.

CASH gets up and pours himself a glass of champagne.

Things are really starting to happen, pal. I lunched Forbert like you said, and the guy is jumping without a parachute. His tongue is so far up my ass he's licking my lips. I don't know what you did over there, Cash, but you've got Buckley and the whole crew creaming themselves. You better think about opening up over here. Better still, get yourself down to Heathrow and come see us. I mean it. So. Call me. And let's bust this thing wide open, OK? They need you. They love you. So come and explore, you hear?

Beat. The machine goes off. CASH raises his glass.

CASH: You got it.

Blackout.

Further titles in the Methuen Modern Plays
series
are described on the following pages.

Methuen's Modern Plays

Jean Anouilh	*Antigone*
	Becket
	The Lark
	Ring Round the Moon
John Arden	*Serjeant Musgrave's Dance*
	The Workhouse Donkey
	Armstrong's Last Goodnight
	Pearl
John Arden and	*The Royal Pardon*
Margaretta D'Arcy	*The Hero Rises Up*
	The Island of the Mighty
	Vandaleur's Folly
Wolfgang Bauer	*Shakespeare the Sadist*
Rainer Werner	
Fassbinder	*Bremen Coffee*
Peter Handke	*My Foot My Tutor*
Frank Xaver Kroetz	*Stallerhof*
Brendan Behan	*The Quare Fellow*
	The Hostage
	Richard's Cork Leg
Edward Bond	*A-A-America!* and *Stone*
	Saved
	Narrow Road to the Deep North
	The Pope's Wedding
	Lear
	The Sea
	Bingo
	The Fool and *We Come to the River*
	Theatre Poems and Songs
	The Bundle
	The Woman
	The Worlds with *The Activists Papers*
	Restoration and *The Cat*
	Summer and *Fables*

Howard Brenton and David Hare	*Brassneck*
	Pravda
Mikhail Bulgakov	*The White Guard*
Caryl Churchill	*Top Girls*
	Softcops and *Fen*
Noël Coward	*Hay Fever*
Sarah Daniels	*Masterpieces*
Shelagh Delaney	*A Taste of Honey*
	The Lion in Love
David Edgar	*Destiny*
	Mary Barnes
	Maydays
Michael Frayn	*Clouds*
	Make and Break
	Noises Off
	Benefactors
Max Frisch	*The Fire Raisers*
	Andorra
	Triptych
Simon Gray	*Butley*
	Otherwise Engaged and other plays
	Dog Days
	The Rear Column and other plays
	Close of Play and Pig in a Poke
	Stage Struck
	Quartermaine's Terms
	The Common Pursuit
Peter Handke	*Offending the Audience* and *Self-Accusation*
	Kaspar
	The Ride Across Lake Constance
	They Are Dying Out
Kaufman & Hart	*Once in a Lifetime, You Can't Take It With You* and *The Man Who Came To Dinner*
Vaclav Havel	*The Memorandum*

Barrie Keeffe	*Gimme Shelter (Gem, Gotcha, Getaway)*
	Barbarians (Killing Time, Abide With Me, In the City)
	A Mad World, My Masters
Arthur Kopit	*Indians*
	Wings
Larry Kramer	*The Normal Heart*
John McGrath	*The Cheviot, the Stag and the Black, Black Oil*
David Mamet	*Glengarry Glen Ross*
	American Buffalo
David Mercer	*After Haggerty*
	Cousin Vladimir and Shooting the Chandelier
	Duck Song
	The Monster of Karlovy Vary and Then and Now
	No Limits To Love
Arthur Miller	*The American Clock*
	The Archbishop's Ceiling
	Two-Way Mirror
	Danger: Memory!
Percy Mtwa	
Mbongeni Ngema	*Woza Albert!*
Barney Simon	
Peter Nichols	*Passion Play*
	Poppy
Joe Orton	*Loot*
	What the Butler Saw
	Funeral Games and The Good and Faithful Servant
	Entertaining Mr Sloane
	Up Against It
Louise Page	*Golden Girls*
Harold Pinter	*The Birthday Party*
	The Room and The Dumb Waiter
	The Caretaker
	A Slight Ache and other plays
	The Collection and The Lover

	The Homecoming
	Tea Party and other plays
	Landscape and *Silence*
	Old Times
	No Man's Land
	Betrayal
	The Hothouse
	Other Places (*A Kind of Alaska, Victoria Station, Family Voices*)
Luigi Pirandello	*Henry IV*
	Six Characters in Search of an Author
Sephen Poliakoff	*Coming in to Land*
	Hitting Town and *City Sugar*
	Breaking the Silence
David Rudkin	*The Saxon Shore*
	The Sons of Light
	The Triumph of Death
Jean-Paul Sartre	*Crime Passionnel*
Wole Soyinka	*Madmen and Specialists*
	The Jero Plays
	Death and the King's Horseman
	A Play of Giants
C. P. Taylor	*And a Nighingale Sang . . .*
	Good
Peter Whelan	*The Accrington Pals*
Nigel Williams	*Line 'Em*
	Class Enemy
Theatre Workshop	*Oh What a Lovely War!*
Various authors	*Best Radio Plays of 1978* (Don Haworth: *Episode on a Thursday Evening;* Tom Mallin: *Halt! Who Goes There?;* Jennifer Phillips: *Daughters of Men;* Fay Weldon: *Polaris;* Jill Hyem: *Remember Me;* Richard Harris: *Is It Something I Said?*)
	Best Radio Plays of 1979 (Shirley Gee: *Typhoid Mary;* Carey Harrison: *I Never Killed My German;* Barrie Keeffe: *Heaven Scent;*

John Kirkmorris: *Coxcombe;* John
Peacock: *Attard in Retirement;* Olwen
Wymark: *The Child*)

Best Radio Plays of 1981 (Peter Barnes:
The Jumping Mimuses of Byzantium;
Don Haworth: *Talk of Love and War;*
Harold Pinter: *Family Voices;* David
Pownall: *Beef;* J P Rooney: *The Dead
Image;* Paul Thain: *The Biggest
Sandcastle in the World*)

Best Radio Plays of 1982 (Rhys
Adrian: *Watching the Plays Together;*
John Arden: *The Old Man Sleeps
Alone;* Harry Barton: *Hoopoe Day;*
Donald Chapman: *Invisible Writing;*
Tom Stoppard: *The Dog It Was
That Died;* William Trevor: *Autumn
Sunshine*)

Best Radio Plays of 1983 (Wally K Daly:
Time Slip; Shirley Gee: *Never in My
Lifetime;* Gerry Jones: *The Angels They
Grow Lonely;* Steve May: *No
Exceptions;* Martyn Read: *Scouting for
Boys*)

Best Radio Plays of 1984 (Stephen
Dunstone: *Who Is Sylvia?;* Don
Haworth: *Daybreak;* Robert Ferguson:
Transfigured Night; Caryl Phillips:
The Wasted Years; Christopher Russell:
Swimmer; Rose Tremain: *Temporary
Shelter*)

Best Radio Plays of 1985 (Rhys
Adrian: *Outpatient;* Barry
Collins: *King Canute;* Martin
Crimp: *The Attempted Acts;*
David Pownall: *Ploughboy
Monday;* James Saunders:
Menocchio; Michael Wall:
Hiroshima: The Movie)

Best Radio Plays of 1986 (*Robert Ferguson: Dreams, Secrets, Beautiful Lies*; Christina Reid: *The Last of a Dyia' Race*; Andrew Rissik: *A Man Alone: Anthony*; Ken Whitmore: *The Gingerbread House*; Valerie Windsor: *Myths and Legacies*